10 PRAISE/WORSHIP CLASSICS FOR SOLO PIANO WITH ACCOMPANIMENT TRAX

I WILL CELEBRATE!

Arranged by
BRUCE GREER

Music Engraved by
RIC SIMENSON

Edited by
CAROL TORNQUIST

Cover Design by
SOUTHERN DRAW DESIGN

Companion Product		
Piano Folio	0 80689 32238 9	301 0162 316
Listening Cassette	0 80689 62434 6	301 0519 508
Listening CD	0 80689 62422 3	301 0519 591
Accompaniment CD	0 80689 64212 8	301 4454 583

Possession of a CCLI license does not give you permission to make any copy of the music contained in this book. If you are unsure as to what rights you do have to copy under a CCLI license or if you want information about CCLI, please call 1-800-234-2446.

WORD MUSIC

IN ASSOCIATION WITH

MARANATHA! MUSIC

> **NOTE:**
>
> The **SOLO PIANO** Section of this folio begins on Page 4 and continues through Page 55.
>
> The optional **SECOND KEYBOARD** section begins on Page 58 and continues through Page 111.
>
> This format makes the book more "user-friendly" ... due to fewer page turns!

© Copyright 2000 Word Music, a division of Word Music Group, Inc.
All Rights Reserved. Printed in U.S.A.

No part of this publication may be reproduced or transmitted in any form or by any means, electronic or mechanical, including photocopy, recording or any information storage and retrieval system, without permission in writing from the publisher.

Printed by Parris Printing, Nashville, TN

CONTENTS

in alphabetical order

	SOLO PIANO	SECOND KEYBOARD
AS THE DEER (with OPEN OUR EYES, LORD)	26	80
BEHOLD, WHAT MANNER OF LOVE (with O HOW I LOVE JESUS)	38	92
COME JUST AS YOU ARE	50	106
HE IS OUR PEACE (with IT IS WELL WITH MY SOUL)	47	103
I WILL CELEBRATE	4	58
JESUS DRAW ME CLOSE (with I AM THINE, O LORD)	15	69
LORD, I LIFT YOUR NAME ON HIGH (with ALL HAIL THE POWER OF JESUS' NAME)	21	75
WE DECLARE YOUR MAJESTY	10	64
YOU ARE MY ALL IN ALL	43	98
YOU'RE WORTHY OF MY PRAISE	33	87

I Will Celebrate
(Solo Piano)

Words and Music by
RITA BALOCHE
Orchestrated by Richard Kingsmore
Arranged by Bruce Greer

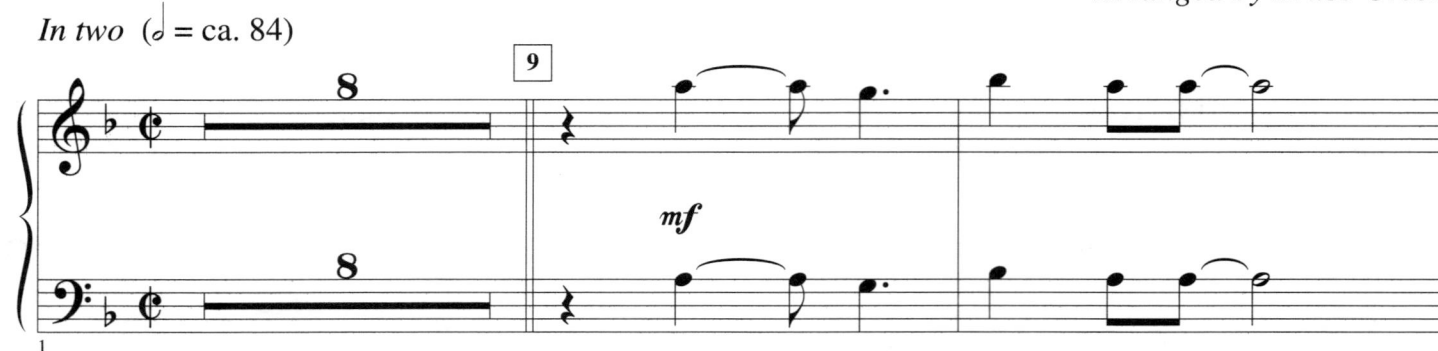

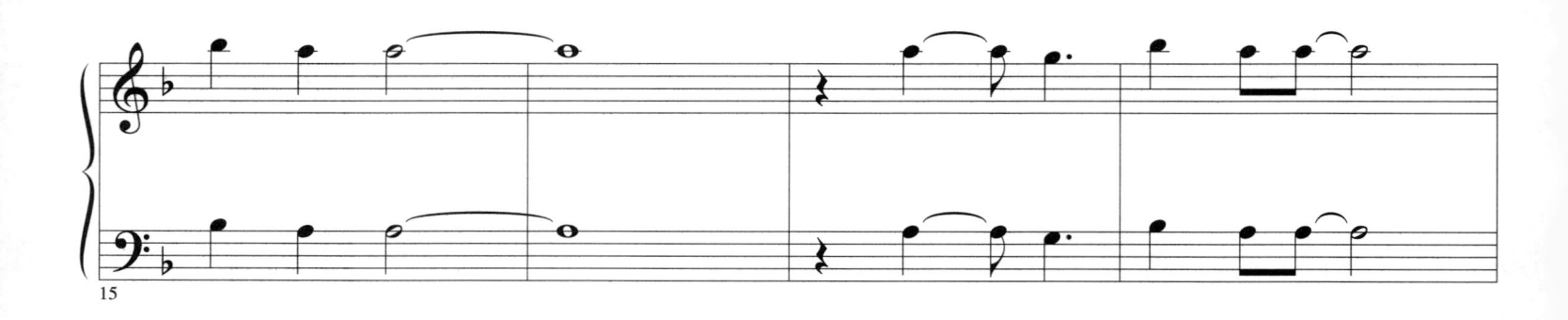

In two ($\bowtie$ = ca. 84)

© Copyright 1990 Maranatha Praise, Inc. (admin. The Copyright Co., Nashville, TN).
All Rights Reserved. Used by Permission.

EVEN IF YOU POSSESS A **CCLI** LICENSE YOU CANNOT COPY ANY MUSIC FROM THIS BOOK.
If you have questions about CCLI, please call 800 / 234-2446.

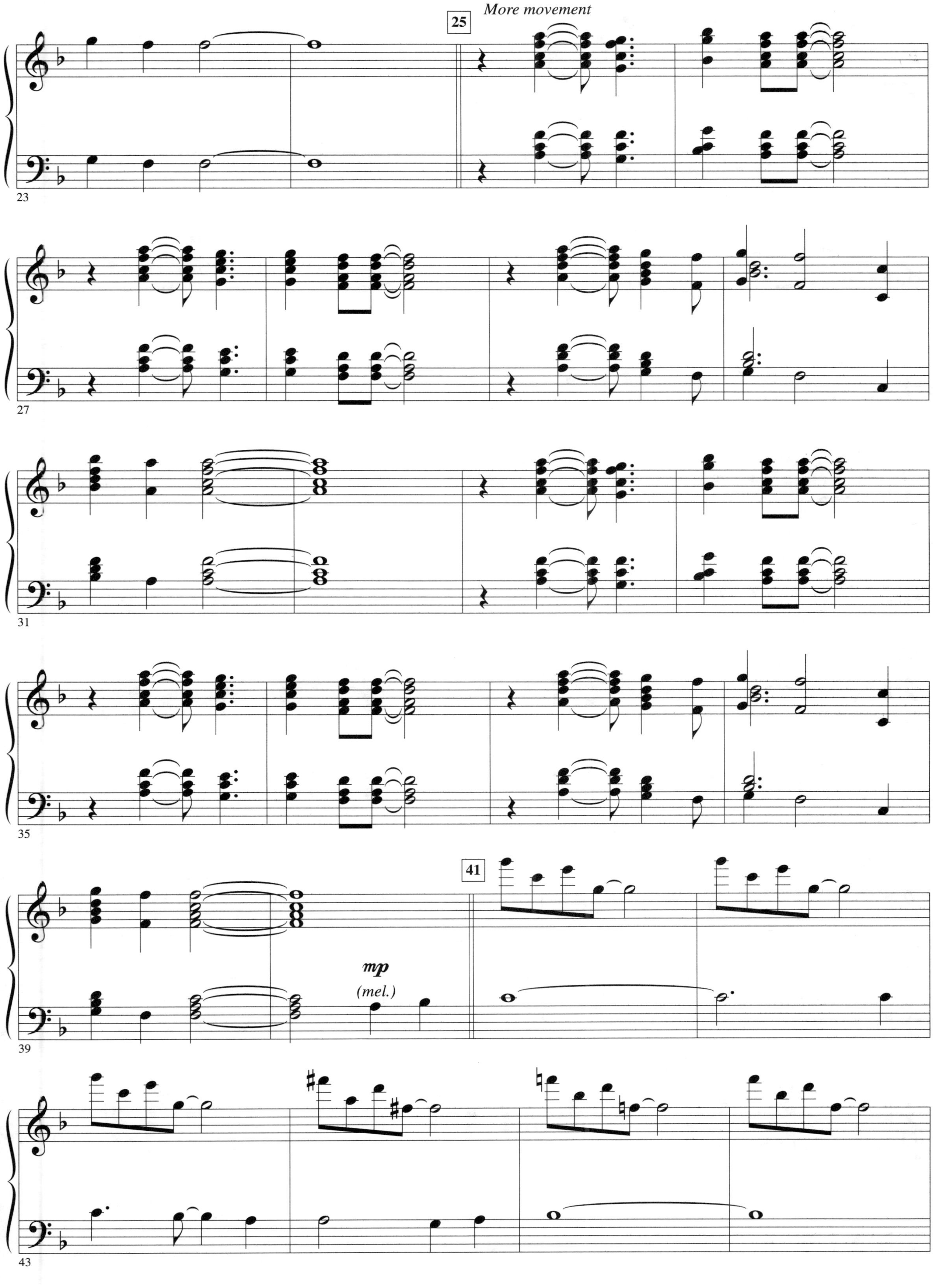
More movement
25
23
27
31
35
41
mp
(mel.)
39
43

6

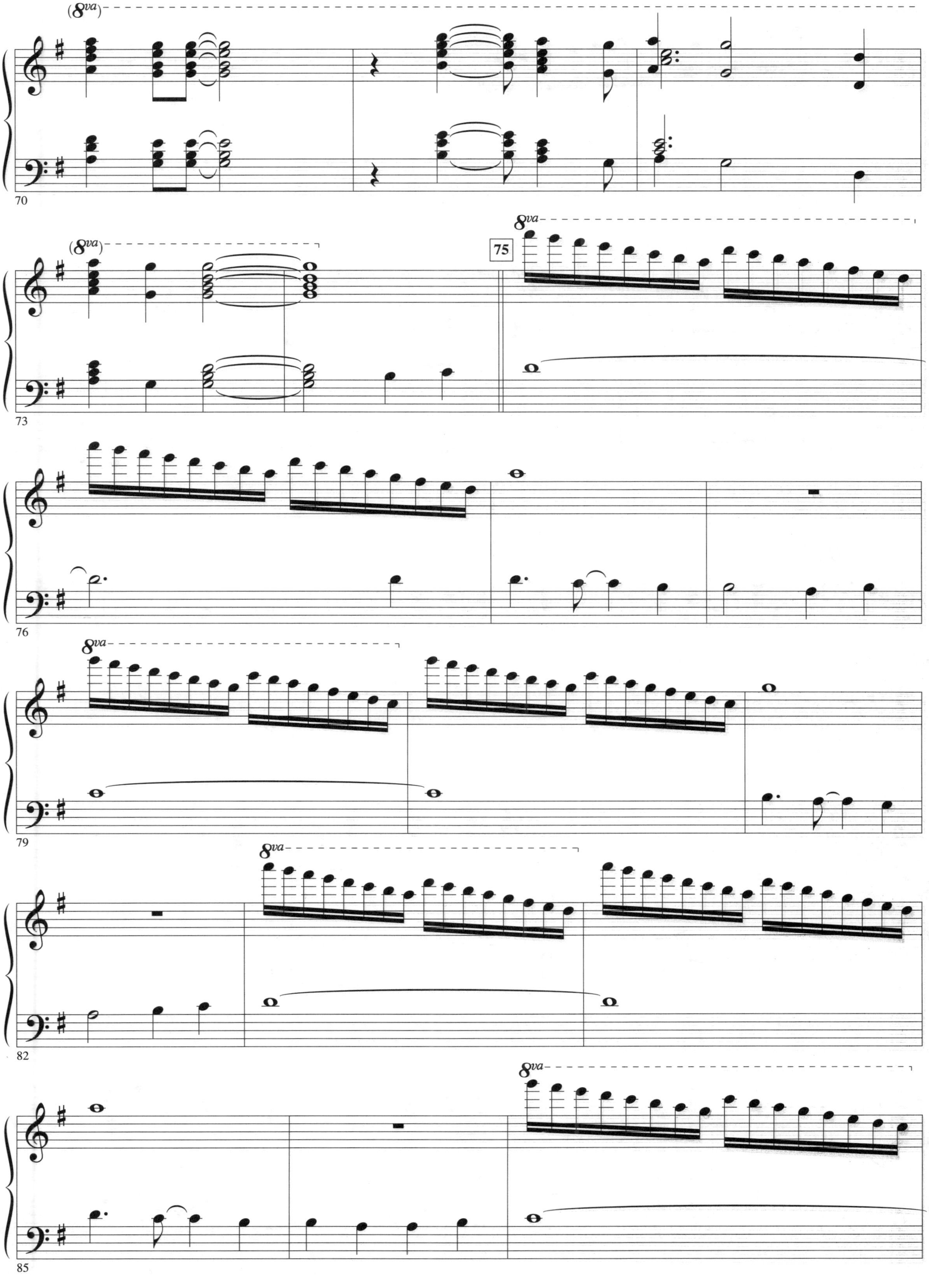
(8va)
70
(8va)
8va
75
73
76
8va
79
8va
82
8va
85

8

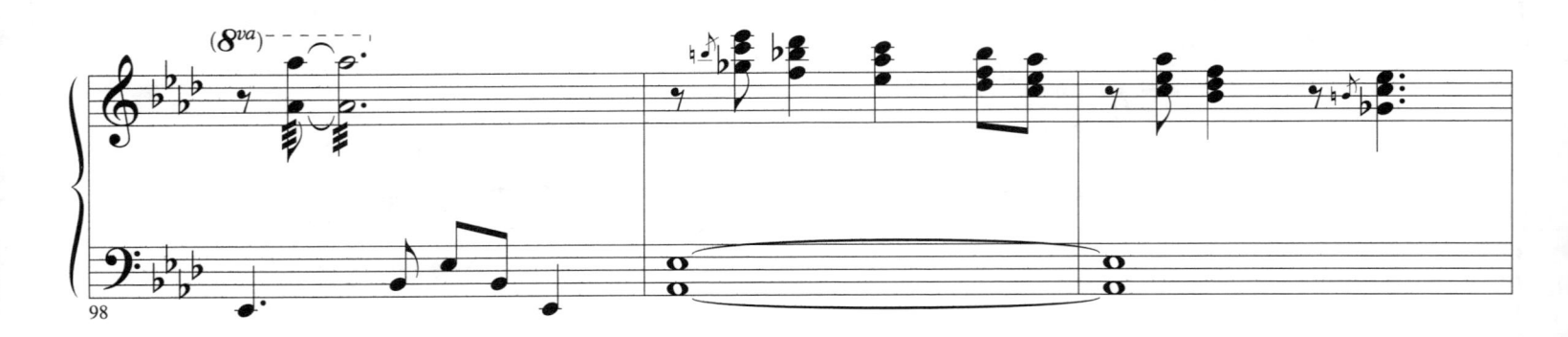

9

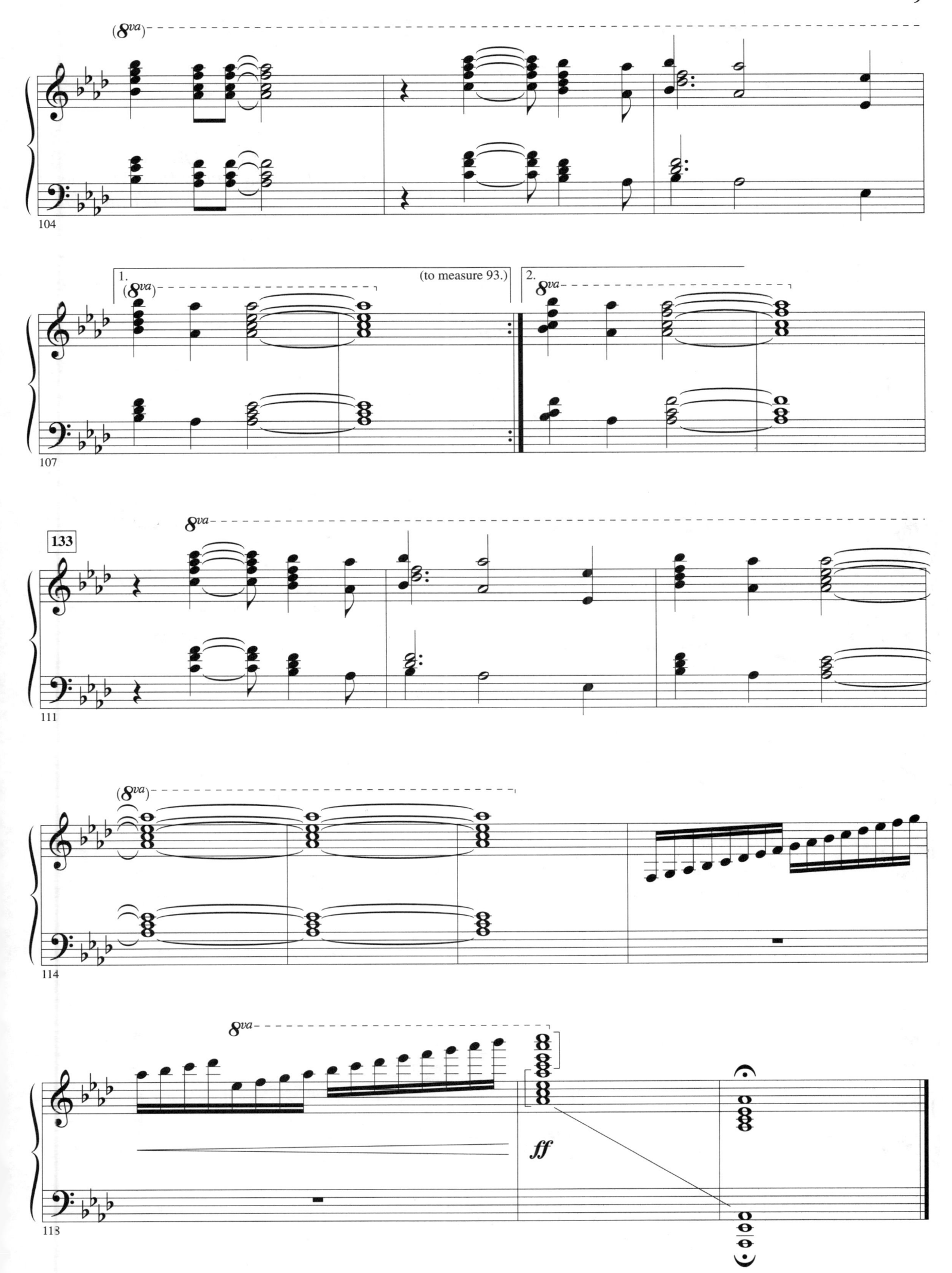

We Declare Your Majesty

(Solo Piano)

Words and Music by
MALCOLM DU PLESSIS
Orchestrated by Dave Williamson
Arranged by Bruce Greer

© Copyright 1985 Maranatha Praise, Inc. (admin. The Copyright Co., Nashville, TN) Except ThankYou Music for Europe.
All Rights Reserved. Used by Permission.

EVEN IF YOU POSSESS A **CCLI** LICENSE YOU CANNOT COPY ANY MUSIC FROM THIS BOOK.
If you have questions about CCLI, please call 800 / 234-2446.

11

12

13

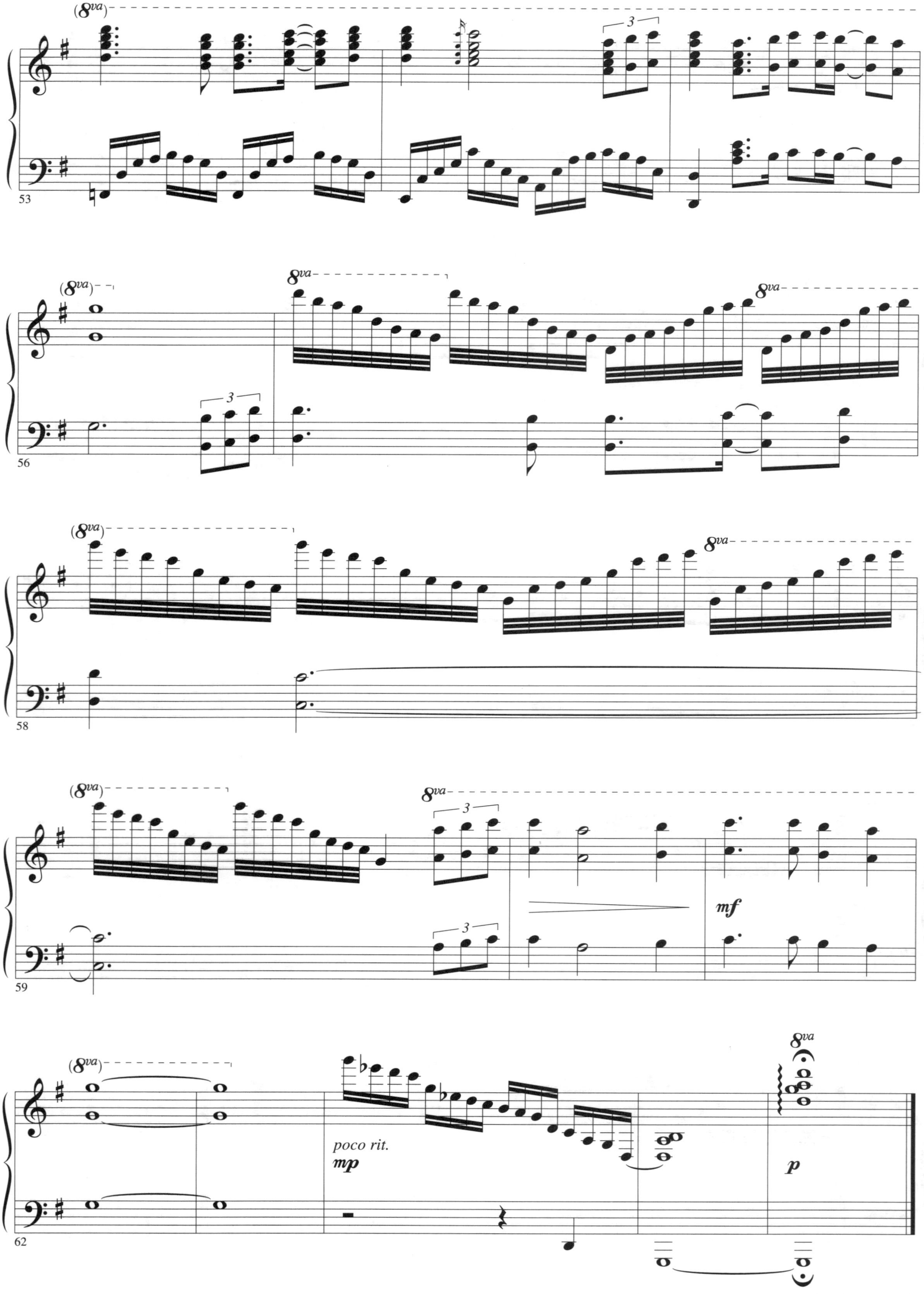
(8va)
3
53
8va
56
58
59
mf
62
poco rit.
mp
p

Jesus, Draw Me Close
with *I Am Thine, O Lord*
(Solo Piano)

Words and Music by
RICK FOUNDS
Track arranged by Gary Rhodes
Arranged and orchestrated by Bruce Greer

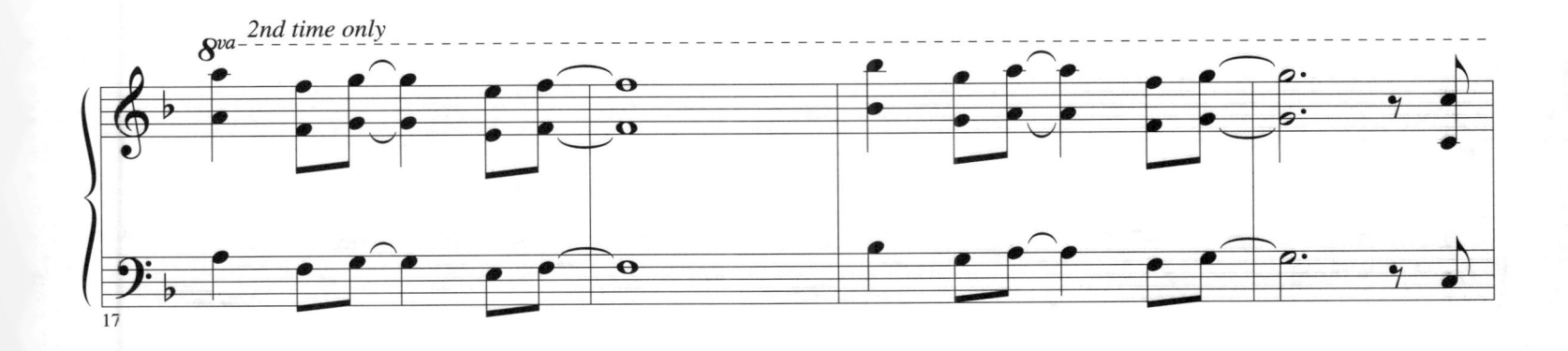

© Copyright 1990 Maranatha Praise, Inc. (admin. The Copyright Co., Nashville, TN).
All Rights Reserved. Used by Permission.

EVEN IF YOU POSSESS A **CCLI** LICENSE YOU CANNOT COPY ANY MUSIC FROM THIS BOOK.
If you have questions about CCLI, please call 800 / 234-2446.

I AM THINE, O LORD *(Crosby/Doane)*

17

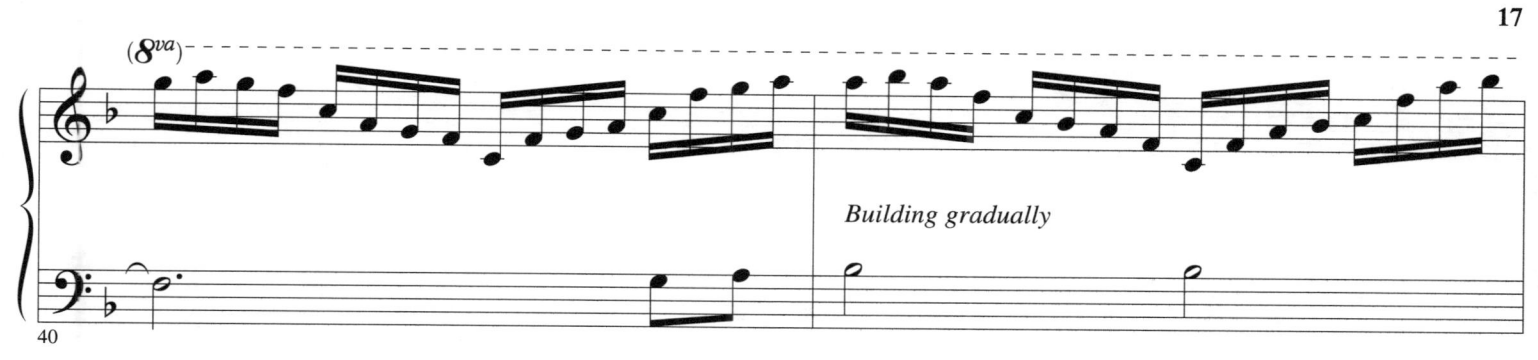

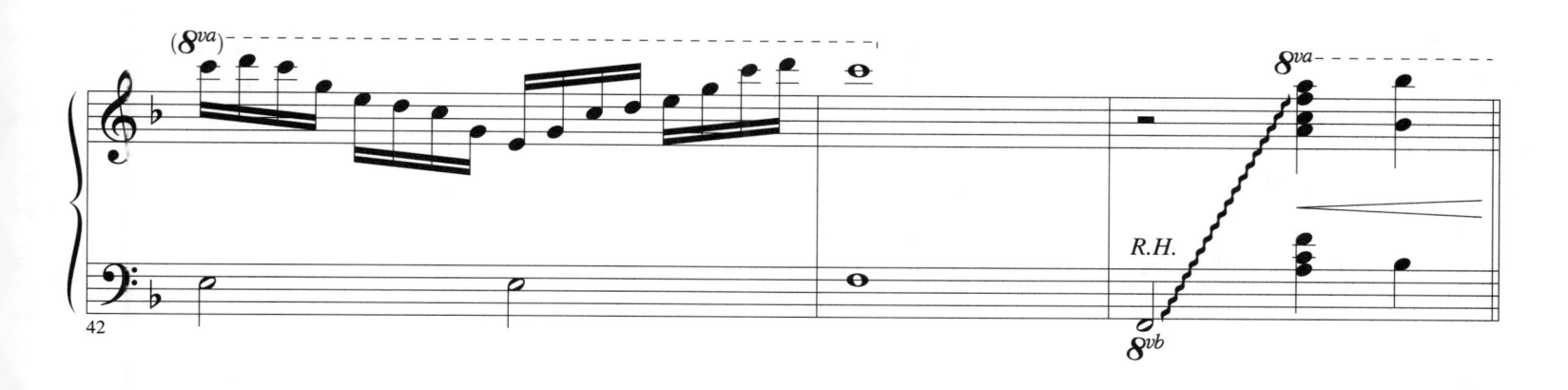

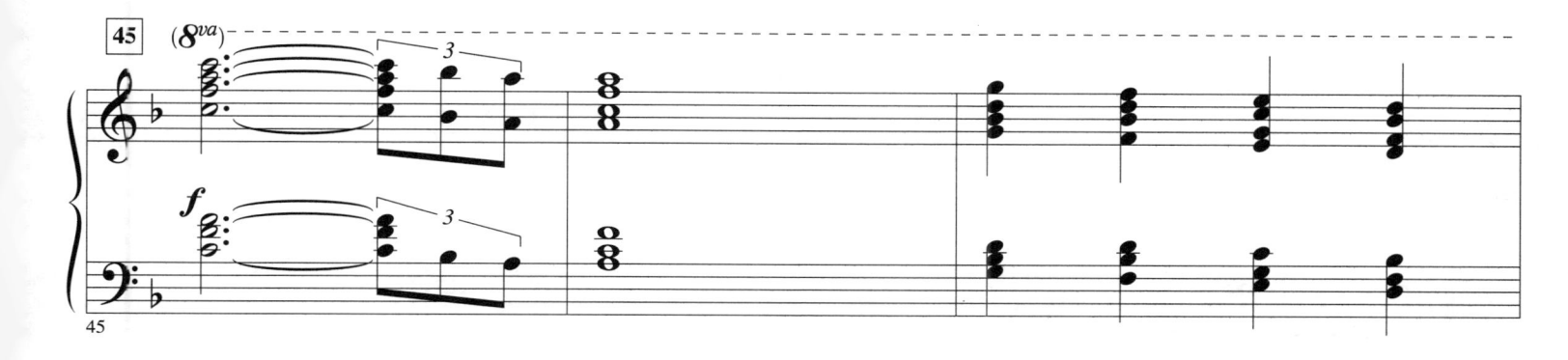

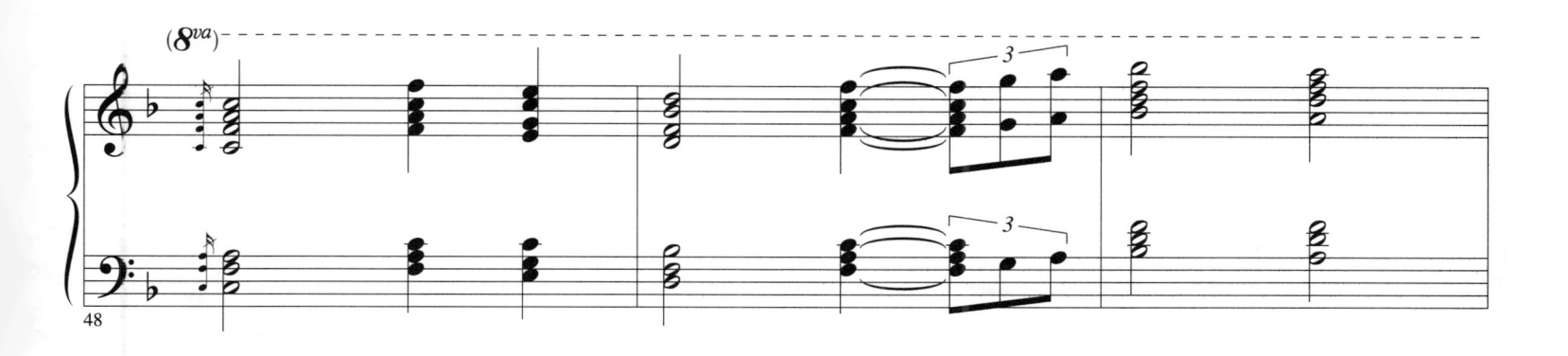

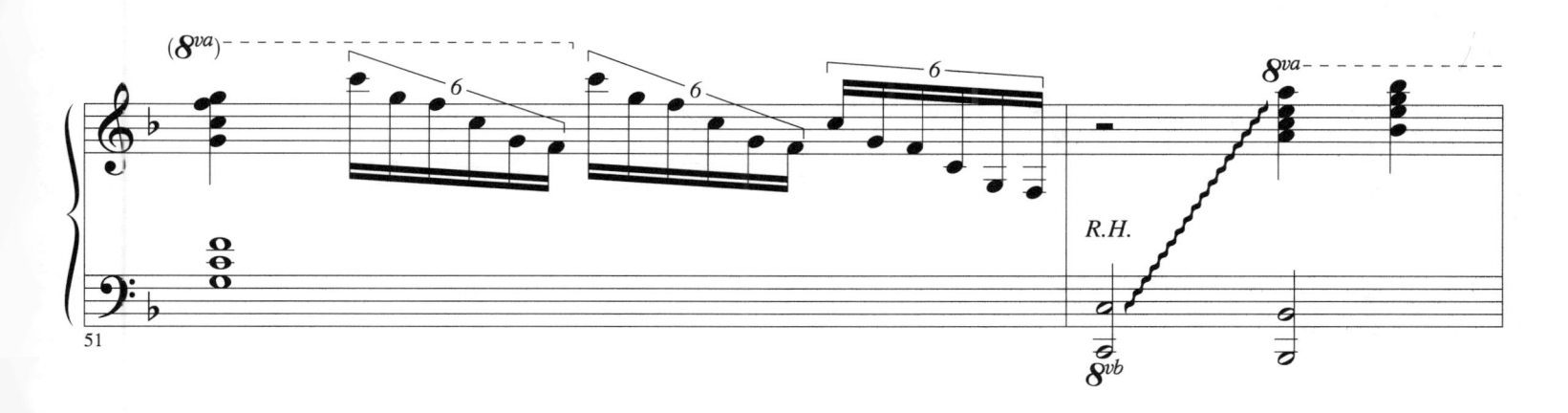

(JESUS, DRAW ME CLOSE)

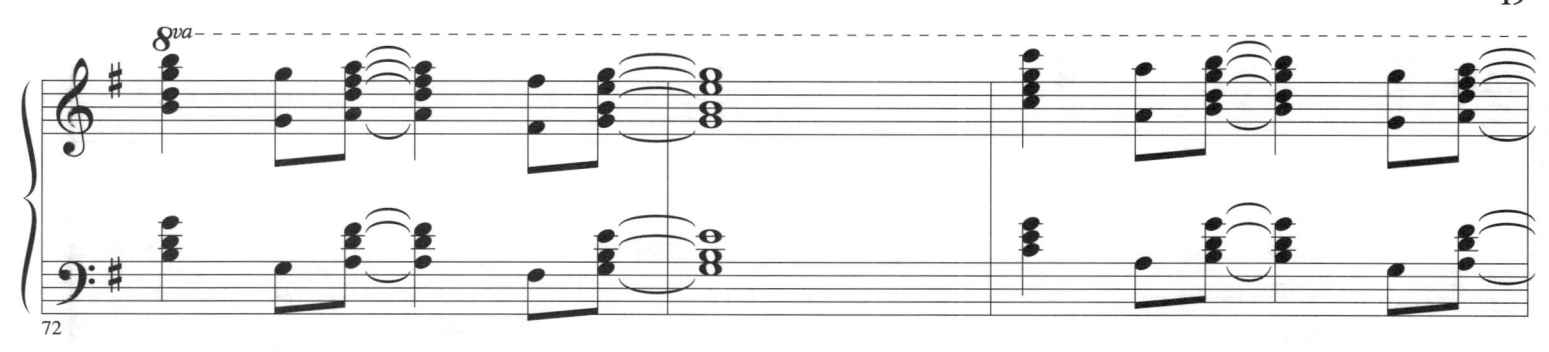

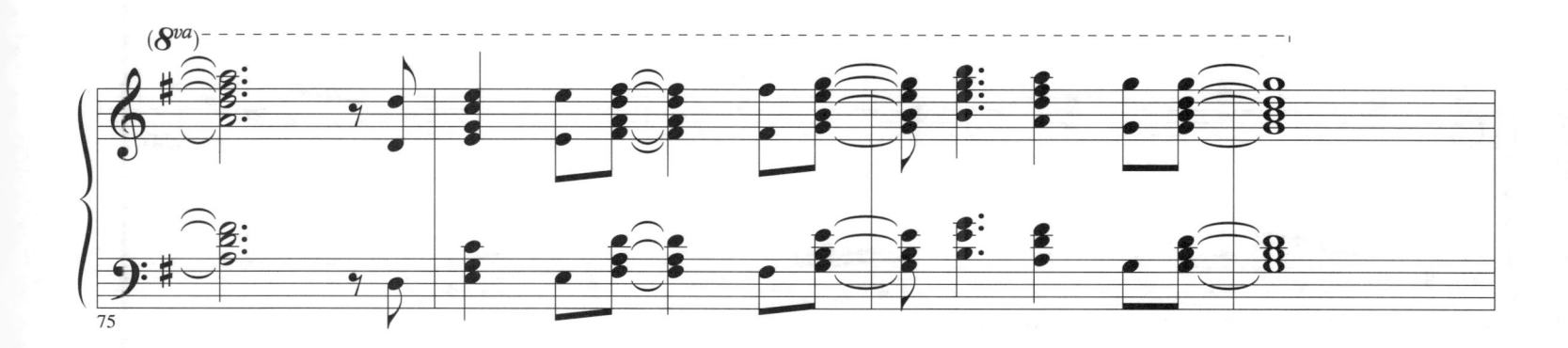

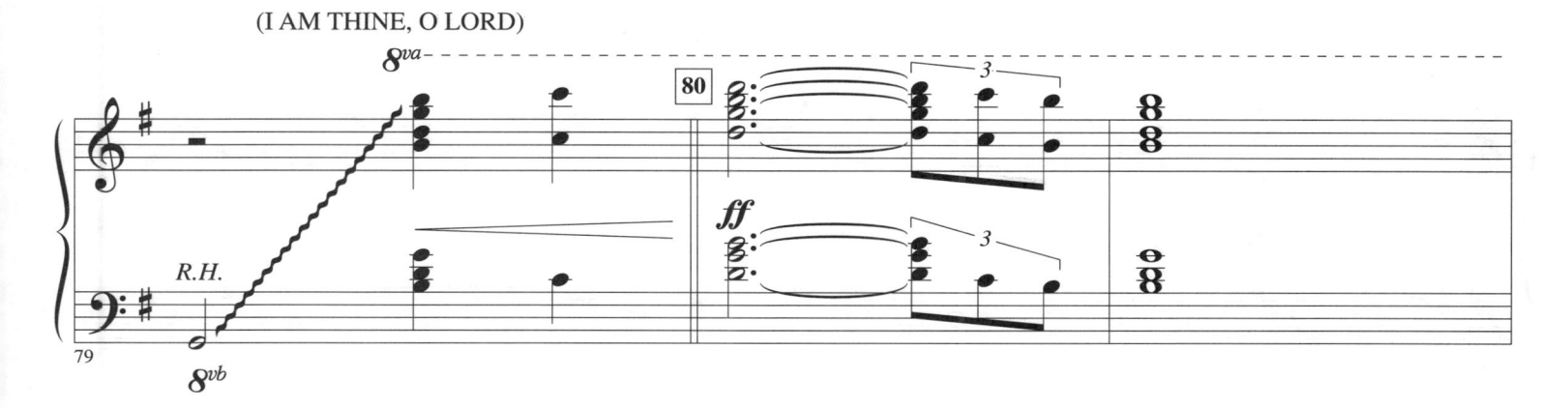

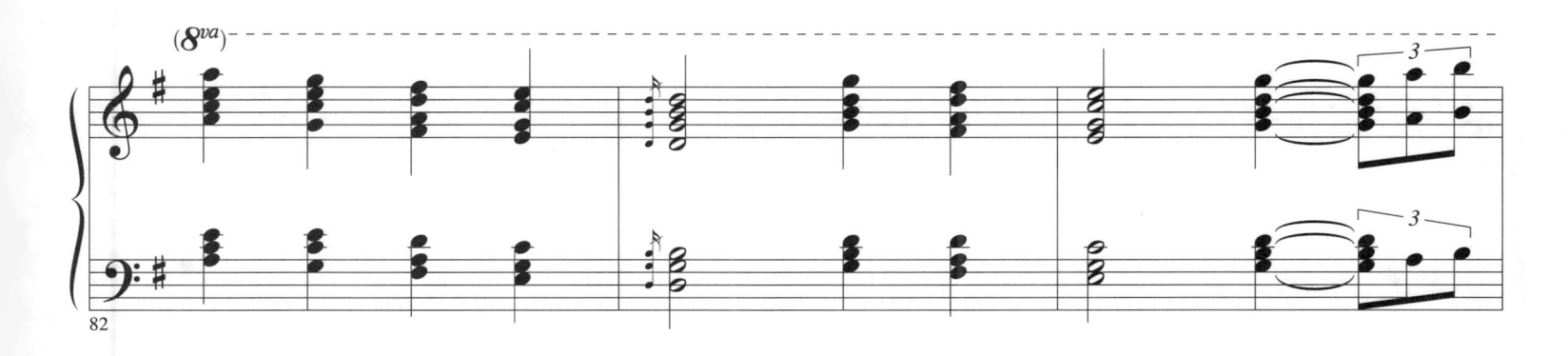

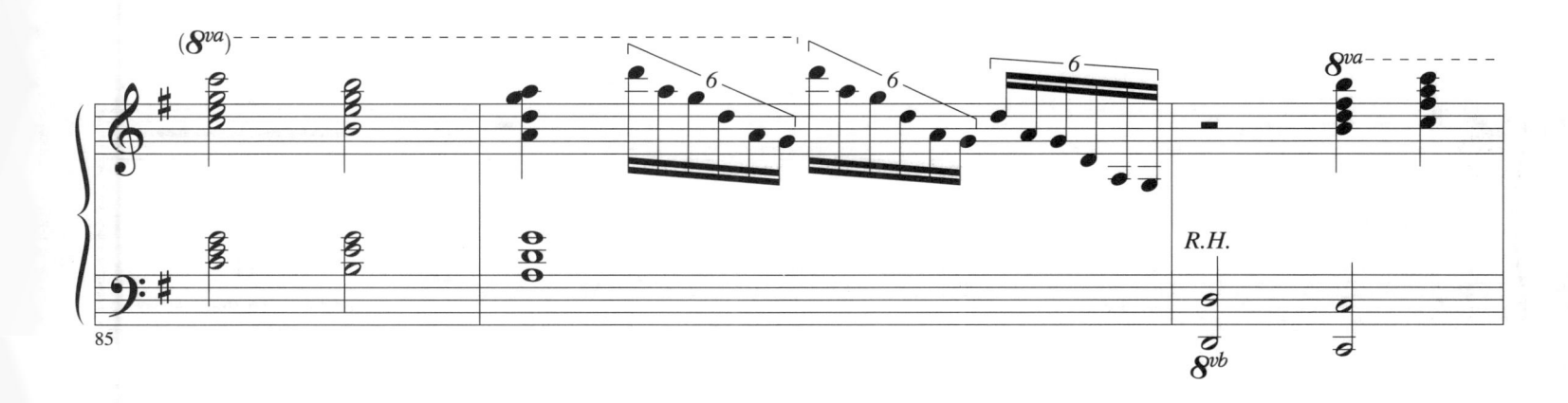

(I AM THINE, O LORD)

(8va)
88
(8va)
90
(8va)
poco rall.
mf
Slightly slower
92
mp
97
slowing
a tempo
6
6
101

Lord, I Lift Your Name on High

with All Hail the Power of Jesus' Name

(Solo Piano)

Words and Music by
RICK FOUNDS
Arranged and orchestrated by Bruce Greer

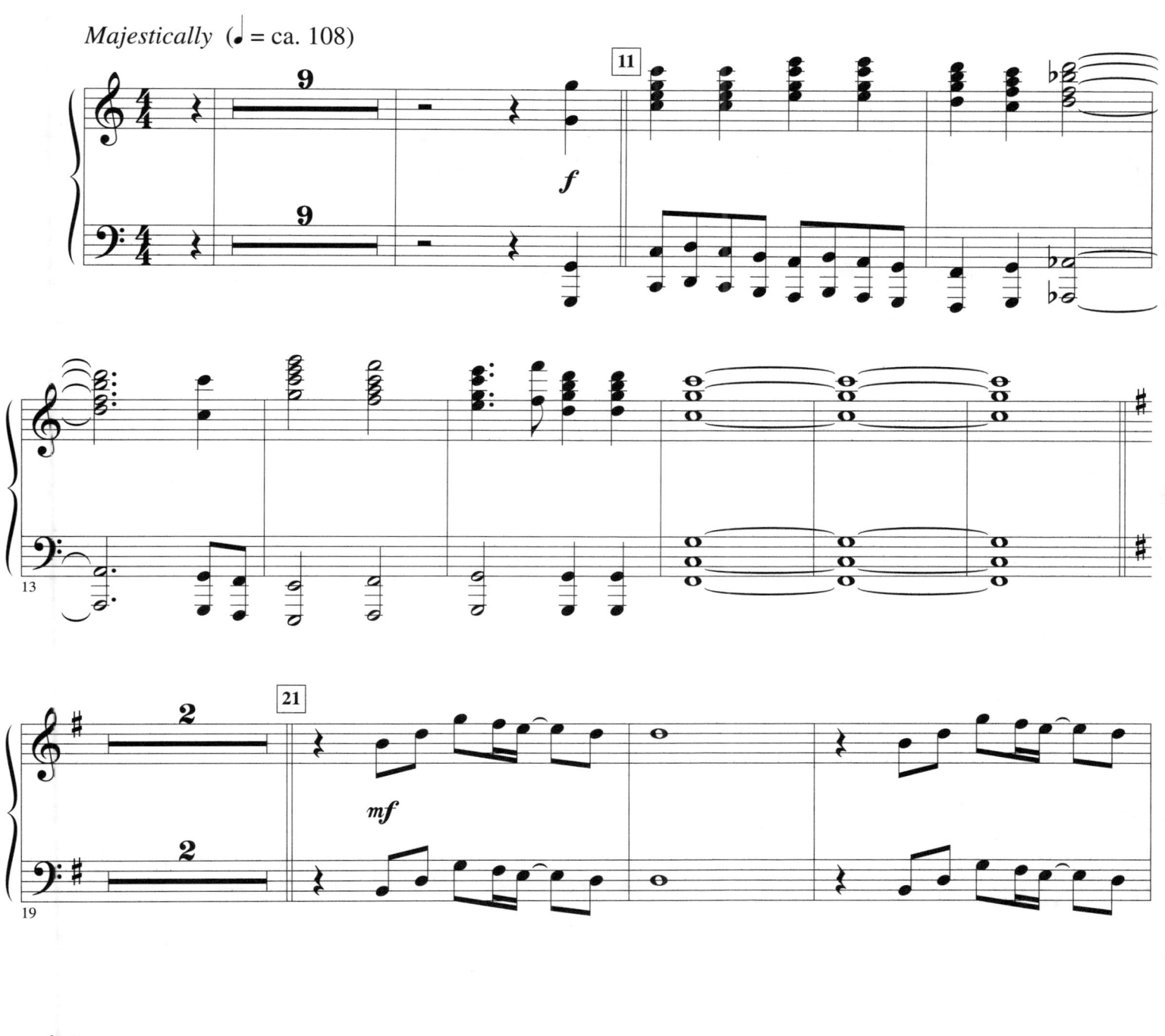

Majestically ($\quarternote$ = ca. 108)

© Copyright 1989 Maranatha Praise, Inc. (admin. The Copyright Co., Nashville, TN).
All Rights Reserved. Used by Permission.

EVEN IF YOU POSSESS A **CCLI** LICENSE YOU CANNOT COPY ANY MUSIC FROM THIS BOOK.
If you have questions about CCLI, please call 800 / 234-2446.

ALL HAIL THE POWER OF JESUS' NAME *(Perronet/Holden)*

(LORD, I LIFT YOUR NAME ON HIGH)

(ALL HAIL THE POWER OF JESUS' NAME)

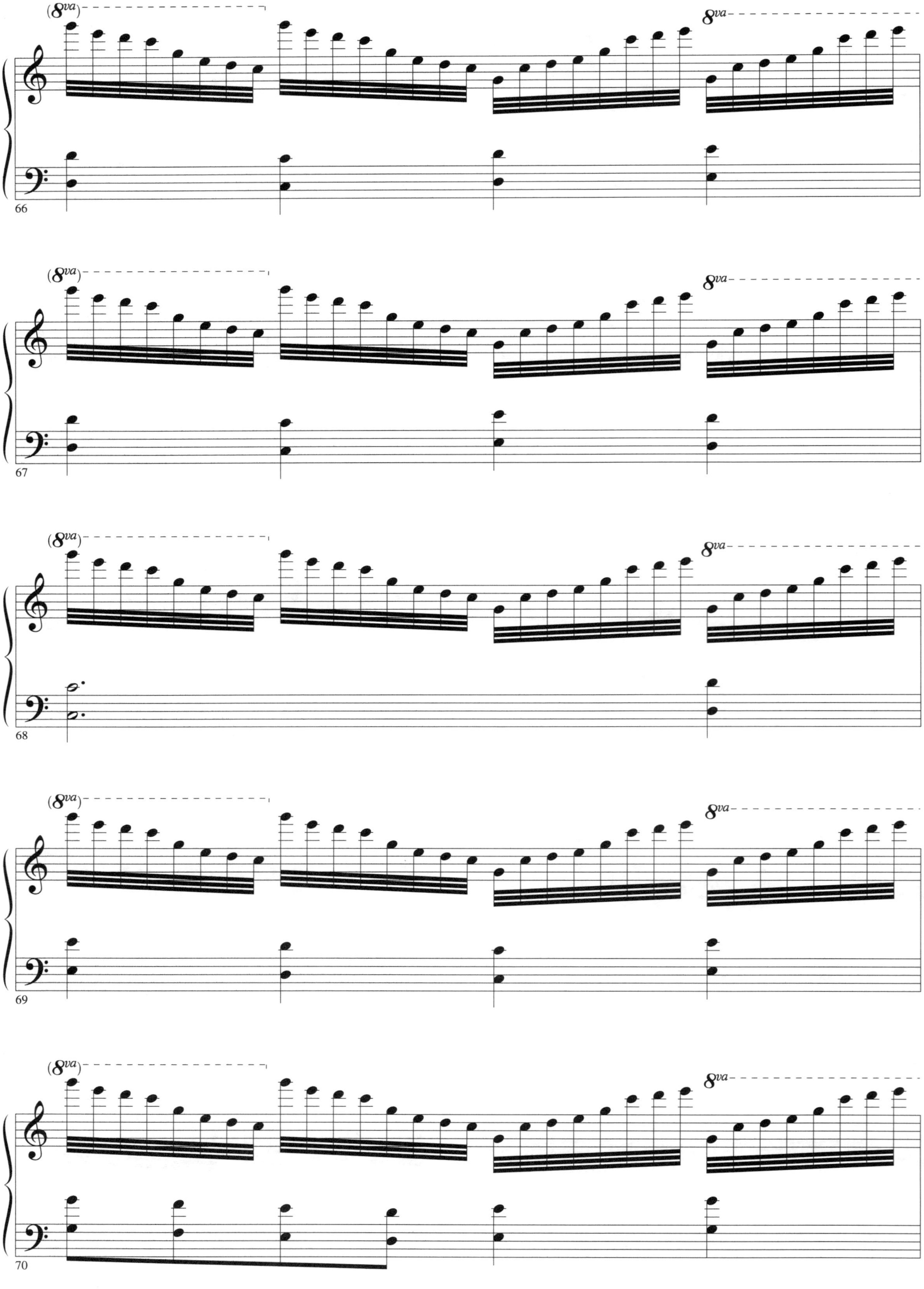
(8va)
8va
66
67
68
69
70

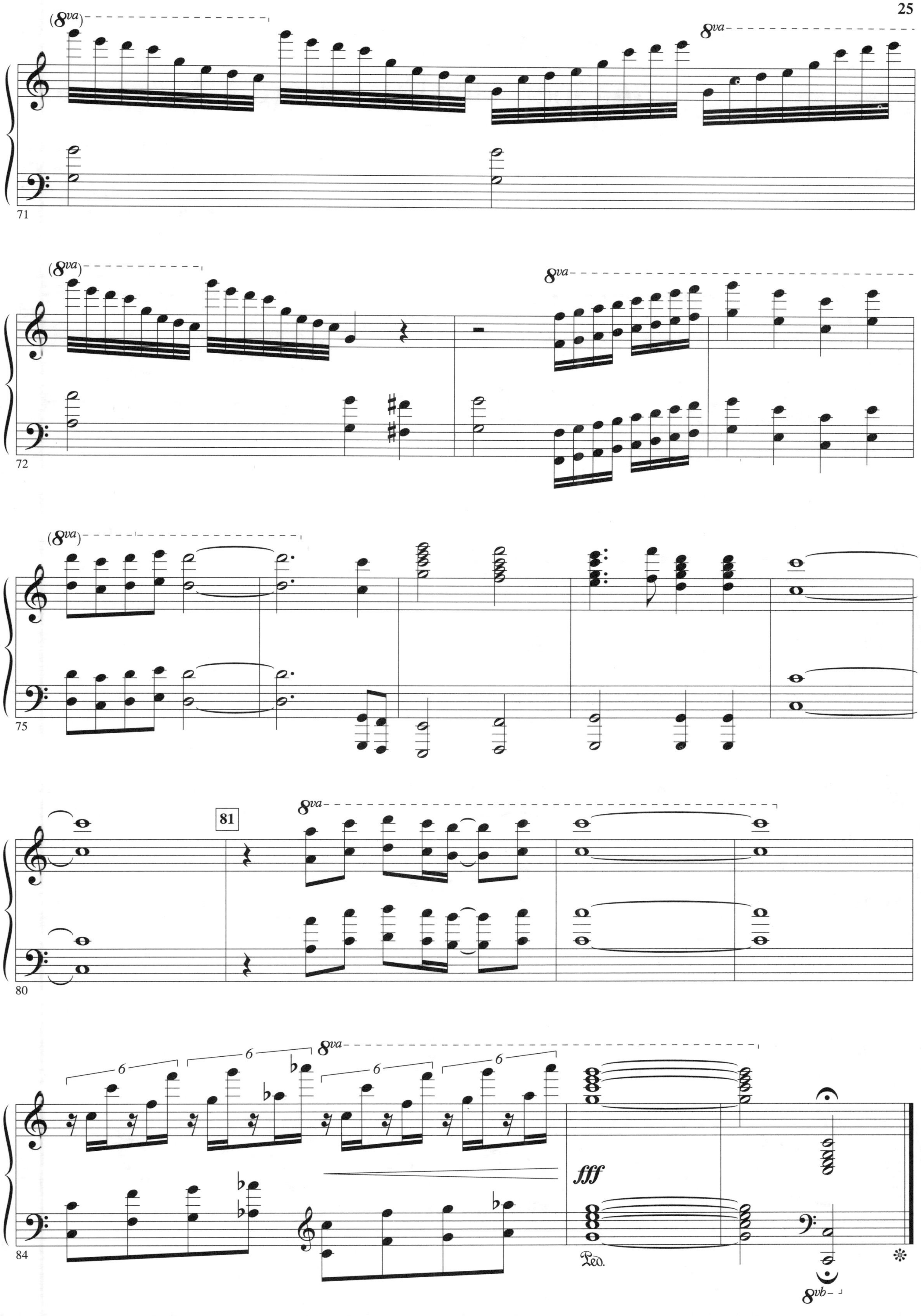
(8va)
8va
71
72
75
80
81
6
fff
Ped.
8vb
84

As the Deer
with Open Our Eyes, Lord
(Solo Piano)

Words and Music by
MARTIN NYSTROM
Orchestrated by Don Hart
Arranged by Bruce Greer

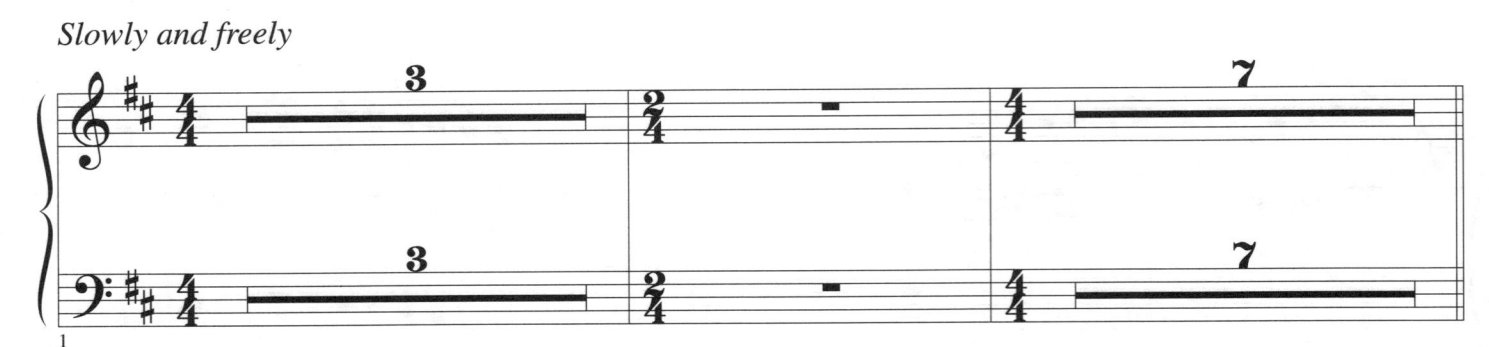

© Copyright 1984 Maranatha Praise, Inc. (admin. The Copyright Co., Nashville, TN).
All Rights Reserved. Used by Permission.

EVEN IF YOU POSSESS A **CCLI** LICENSE YOU CANNOT COPY ANY MUSIC FROM THIS BOOK.
If you have questions about CCLI, please call 800 / 234-2446.

27

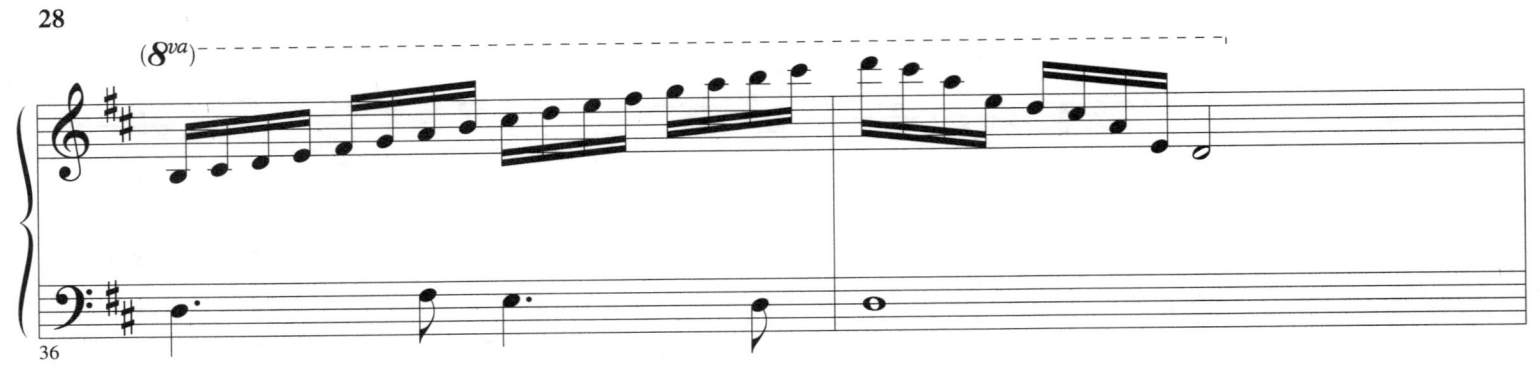

OPEN OUR EYES, LORD *(Robert Cull)*
Moderately fast tempo (♩ = ca. 93)

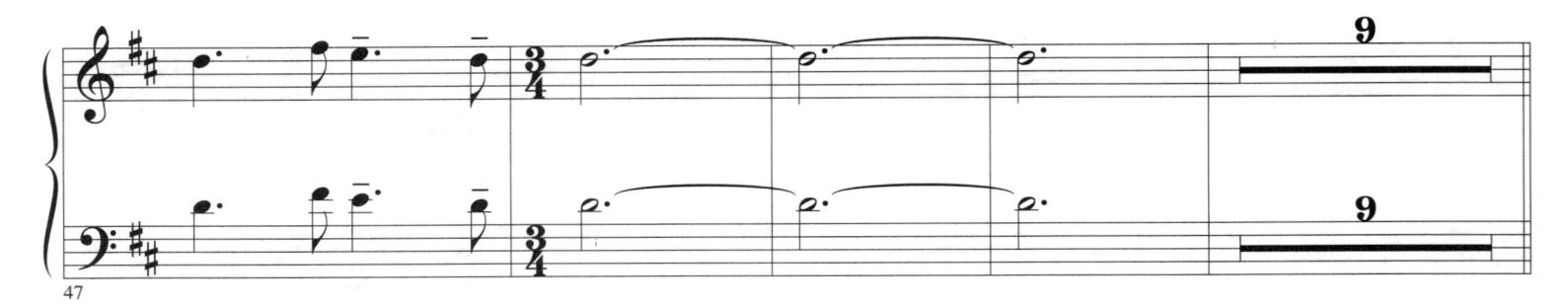

© Copyright 1976 Maranatha Music (admin. The Copyright Co., Nashville, TN). All Rights Reserved. Used by Permission.

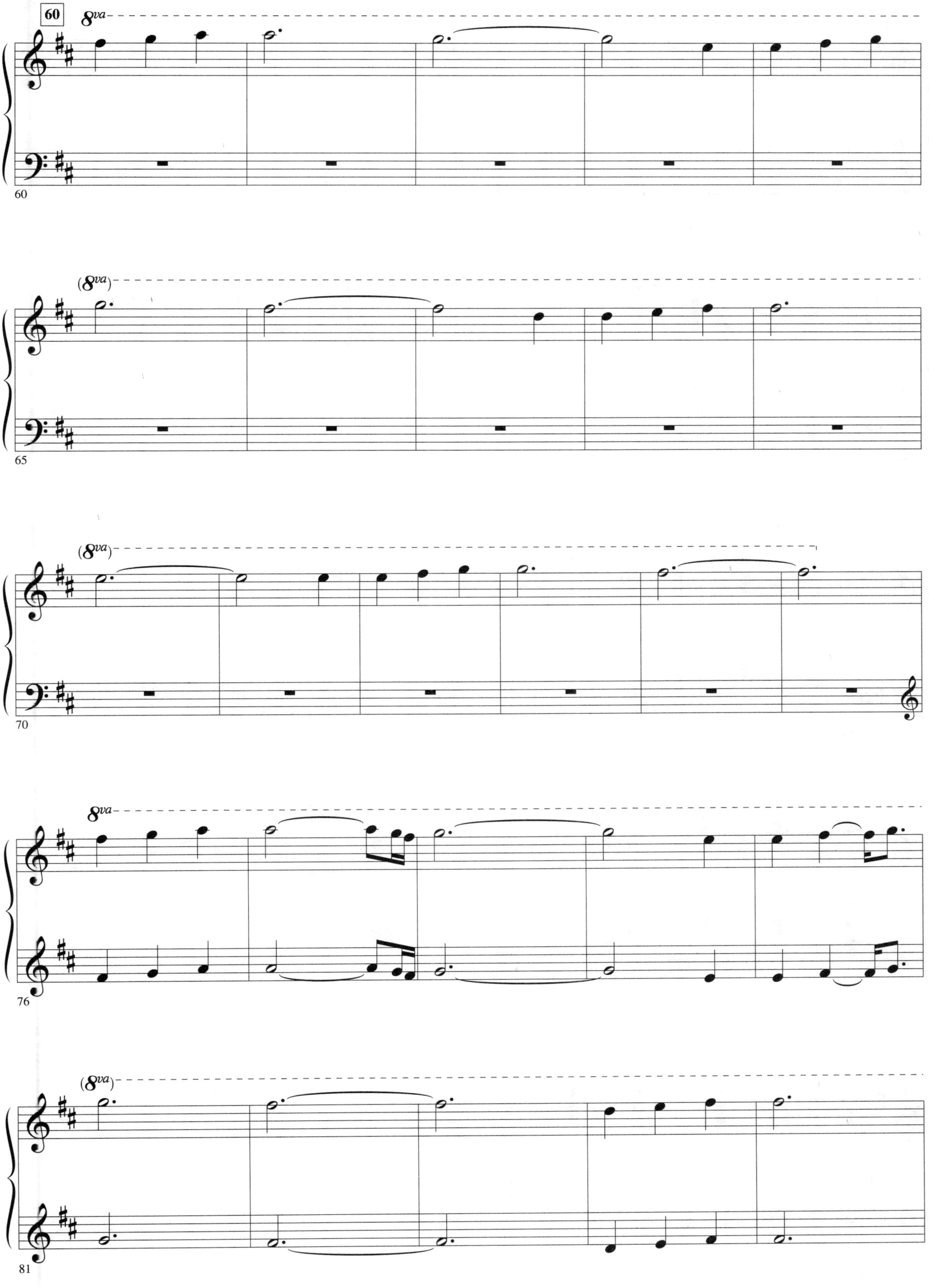
60
8va
60
(8va)
65
(8va)
70
8va
76
(8va)
81

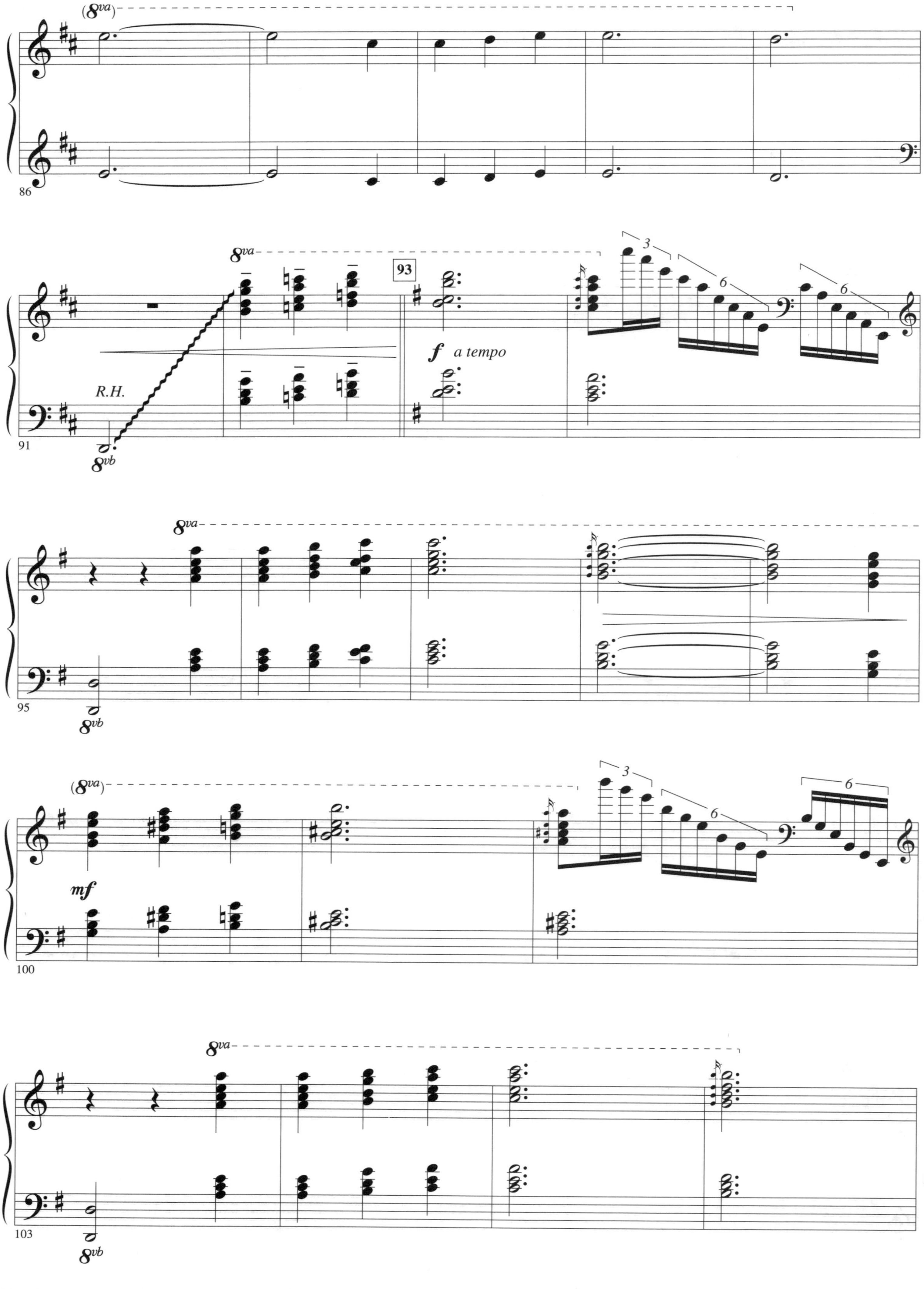
(8va)
86
8va
R.H.
8vb
91
93
f a tempo
3
6
6
8va
95
8vb
(8va)
mf
3
6
6
100
8va
103
8vb

31

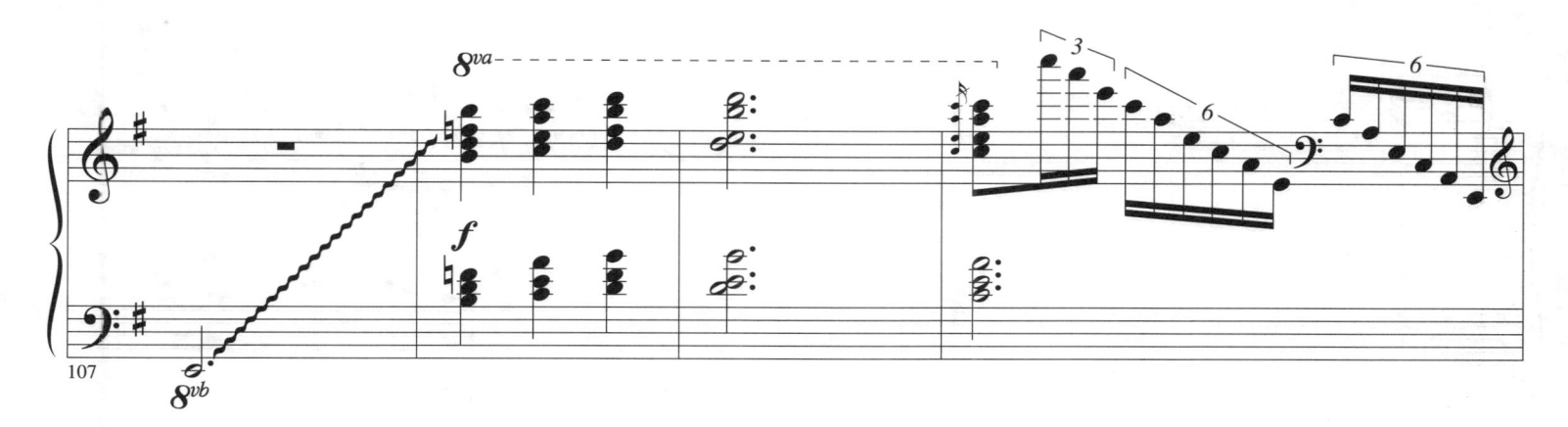

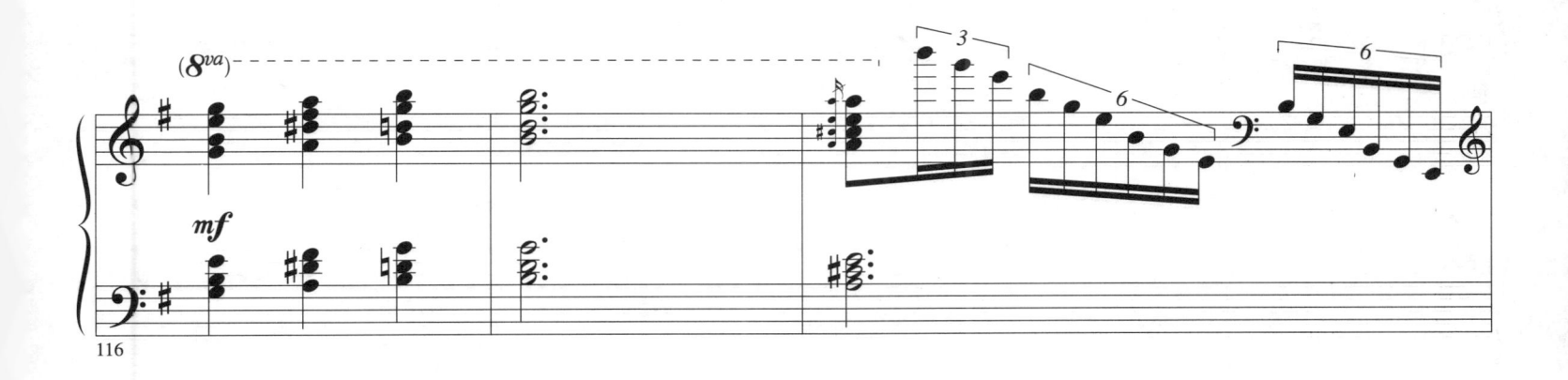

(AS THE DEER) (♩ = ca. 74)
Broadly

You're Worthy of My Praise
(Solo Piano)

Words and Music by
DAVID RUIS
Orchestrated by Don Hart
Arranged by Bruce Greer

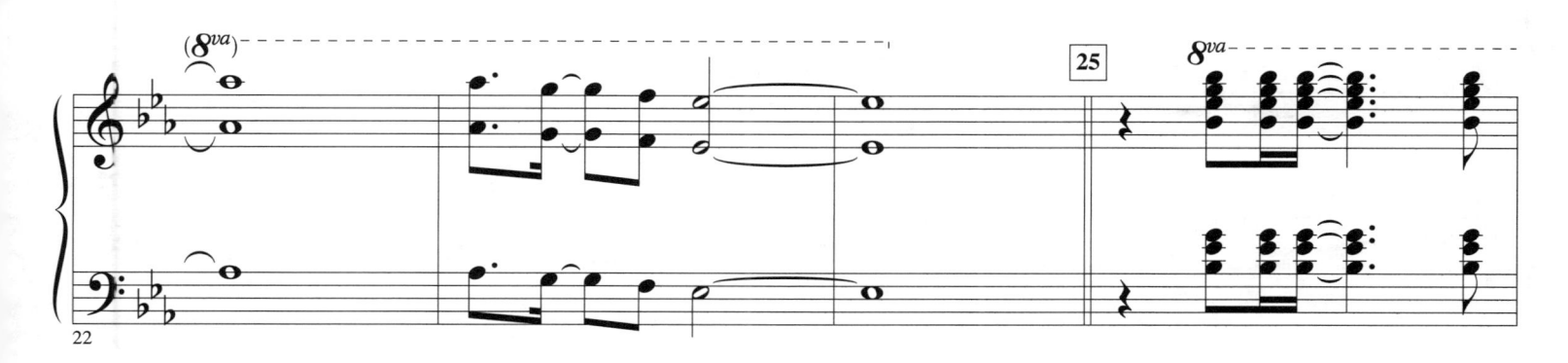

Steady four (♩ = ca. 91)

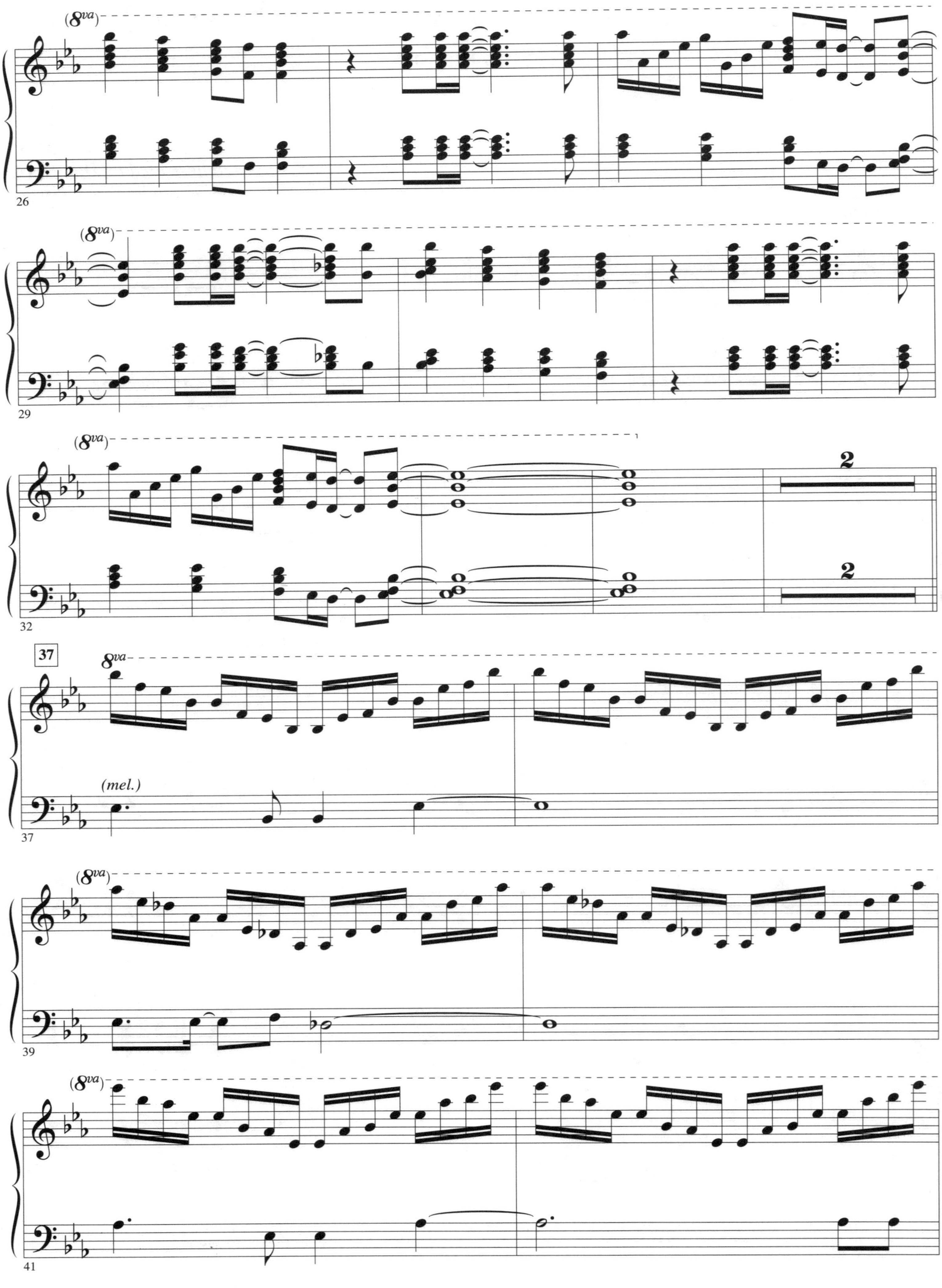
(8va)
26
(8va)
29
(8va)
2
2
32
37
8va
(mel.)
37
(8va)
39
(8va)
41

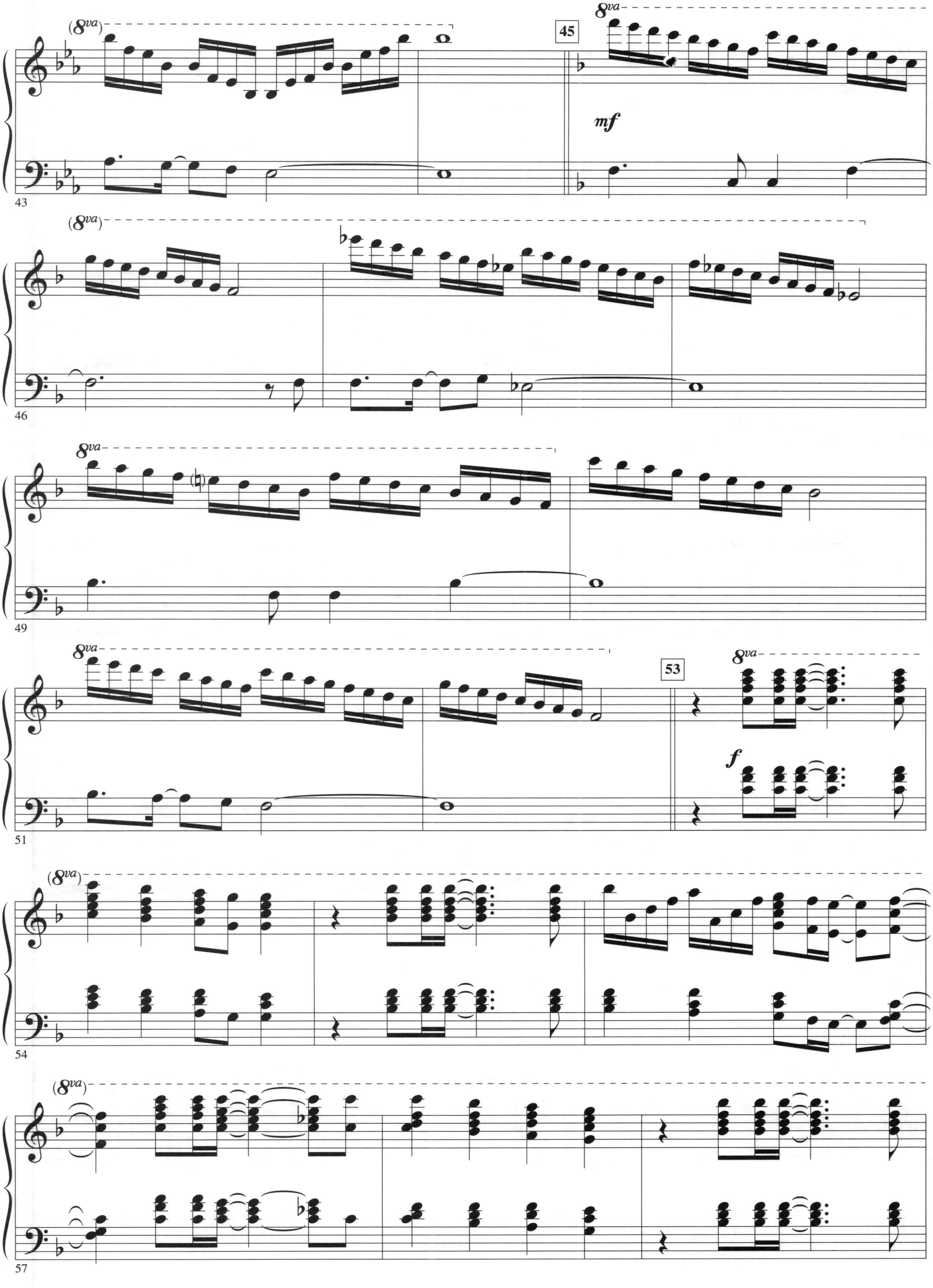
(8va)
45
8va
mf
43
(8va)
46
8va
49
8va
53
8va
f
51
(8va)
54
(8va)
57

36

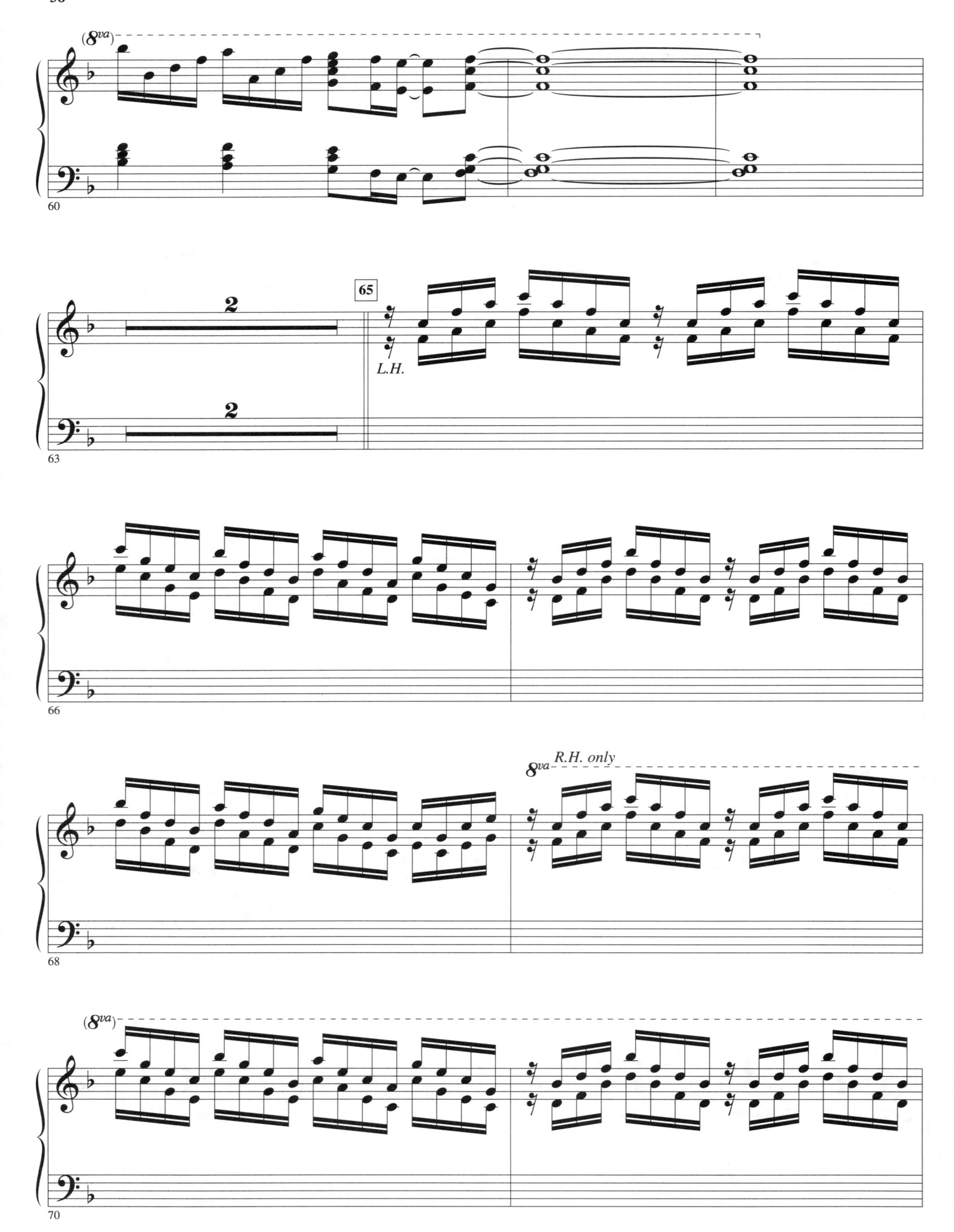

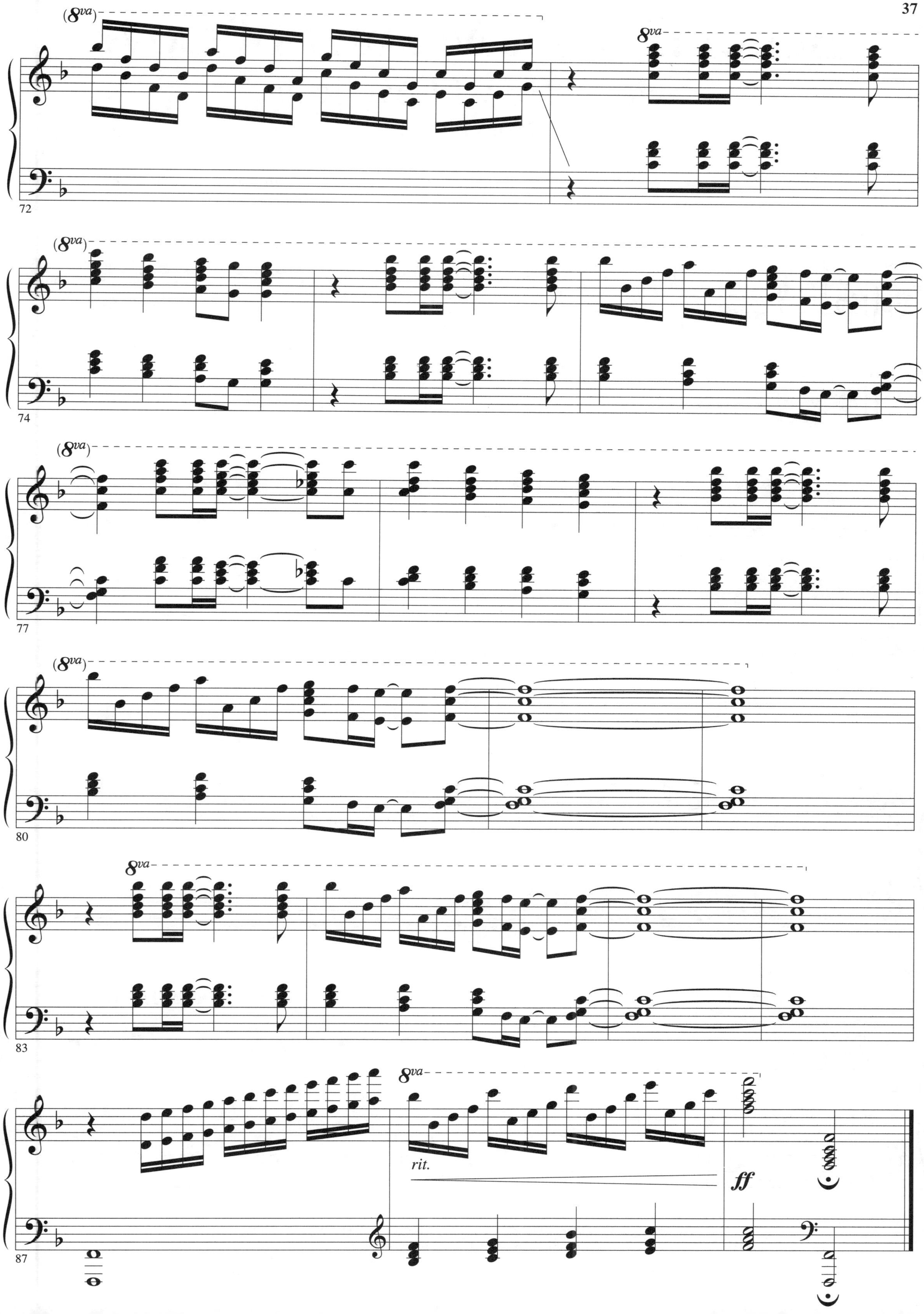
(8va)
8va
72
(8va)
74
(8va)
77
(8va)
80
8va
83
8va
rit.
ff
87

Behold, What Manner of Love
with O How I Love Jesus
(Solo Piano)

Words and Music by
PATRICIA VAN TINE
Arranged and orchestrated by Bruce Greer

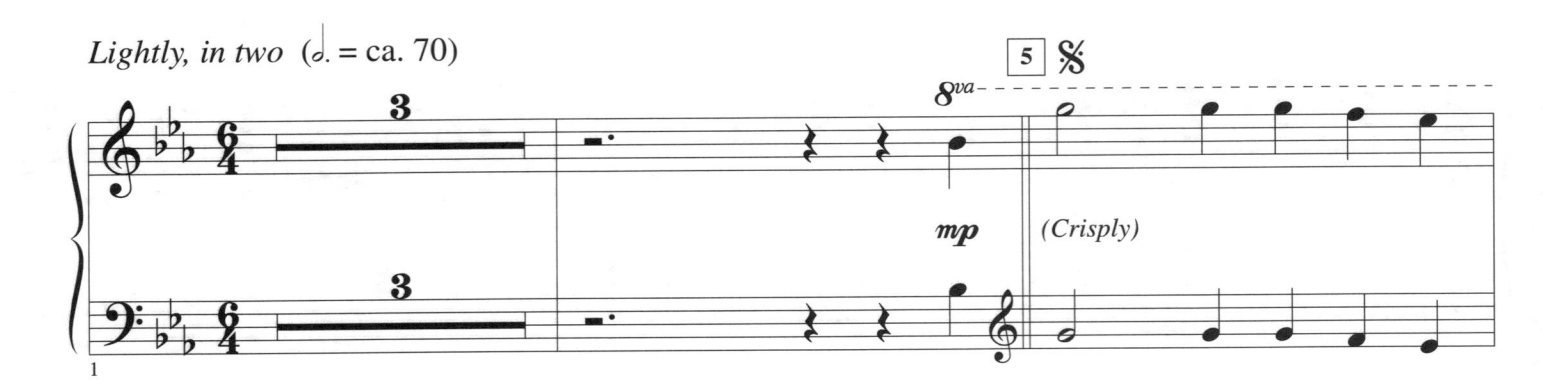

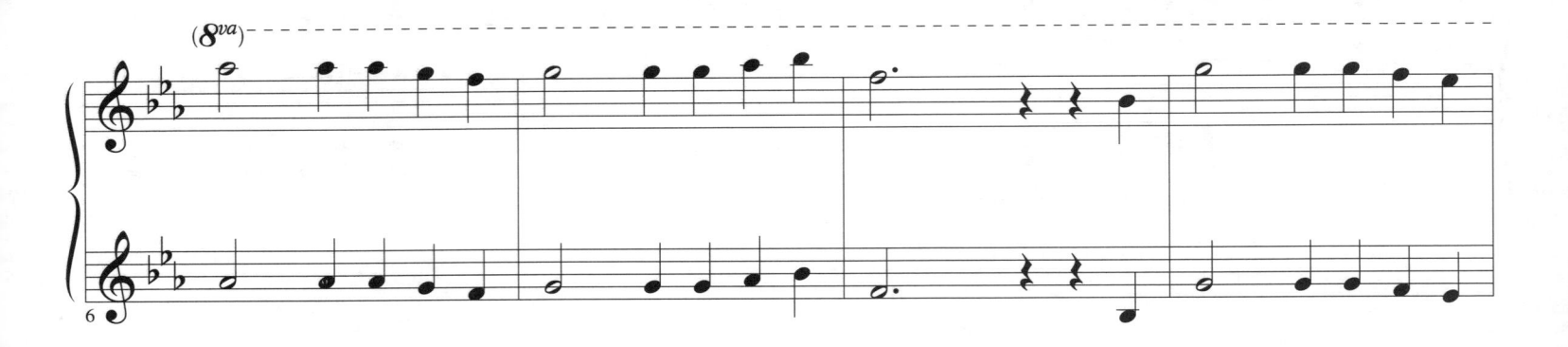

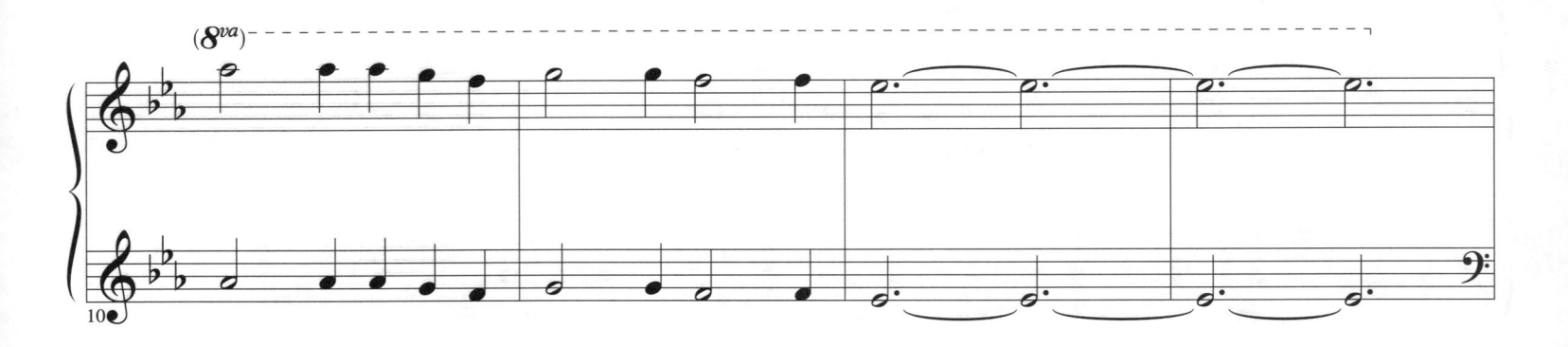

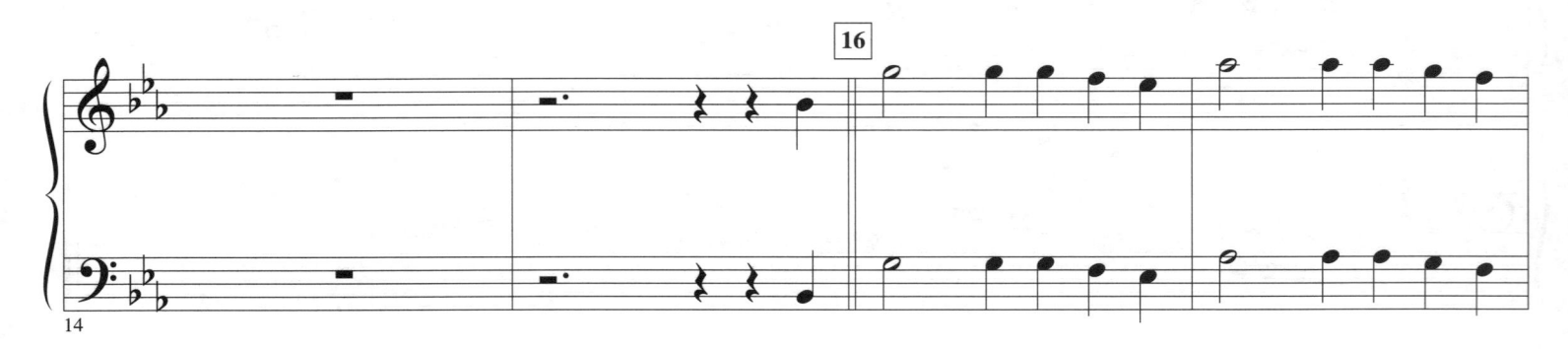

Lightly, in two (♩. = ca. 70)

© Copyright 1978 Maranatha! Music (admin. The Copyright Co., Nashville, TN).
All Rights Reserved. Used by Permission.

EVEN IF YOU POSSESS A **CCLI** LICENSE YOU CANNOT COPY ANY MUSIC FROM THIS BOOK.
If you have questions about CCLI, please call 800 / 234-2446.

O HOW I LOVE JESUS
(Whitfield/Traditional American melody)

Arr. © Copyright 1995 Maranatha! Music (admin. The Copyright Co., Nashville, TN). All Rights Reserved. Used by Permission.

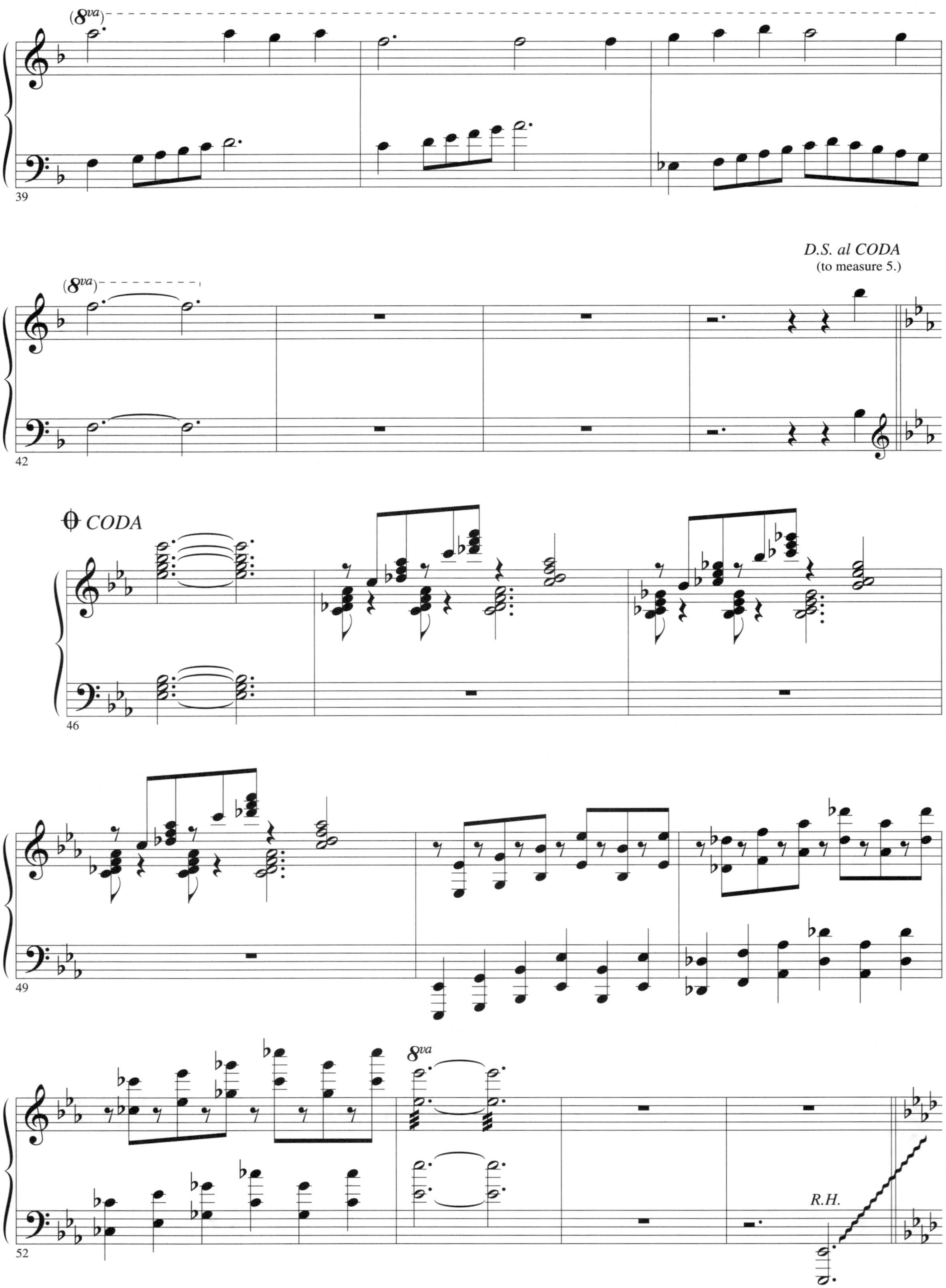
(8va)
39
(8va)
D.S. al CODA
(to measure 5.)
42
CODA
46
49
8va
R.H.
52

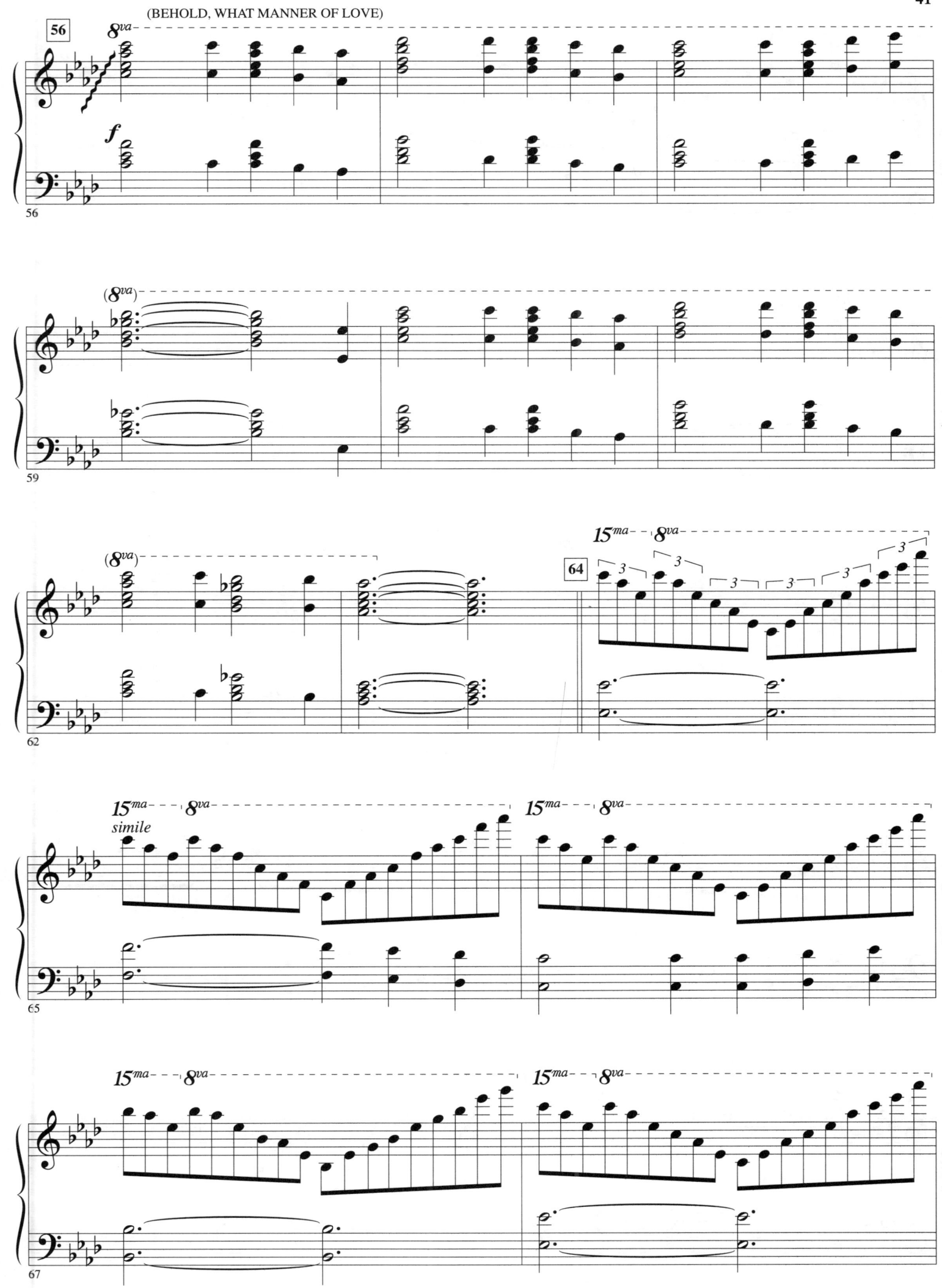

(BEHOLD, WHAT MANNER OF LOVE)

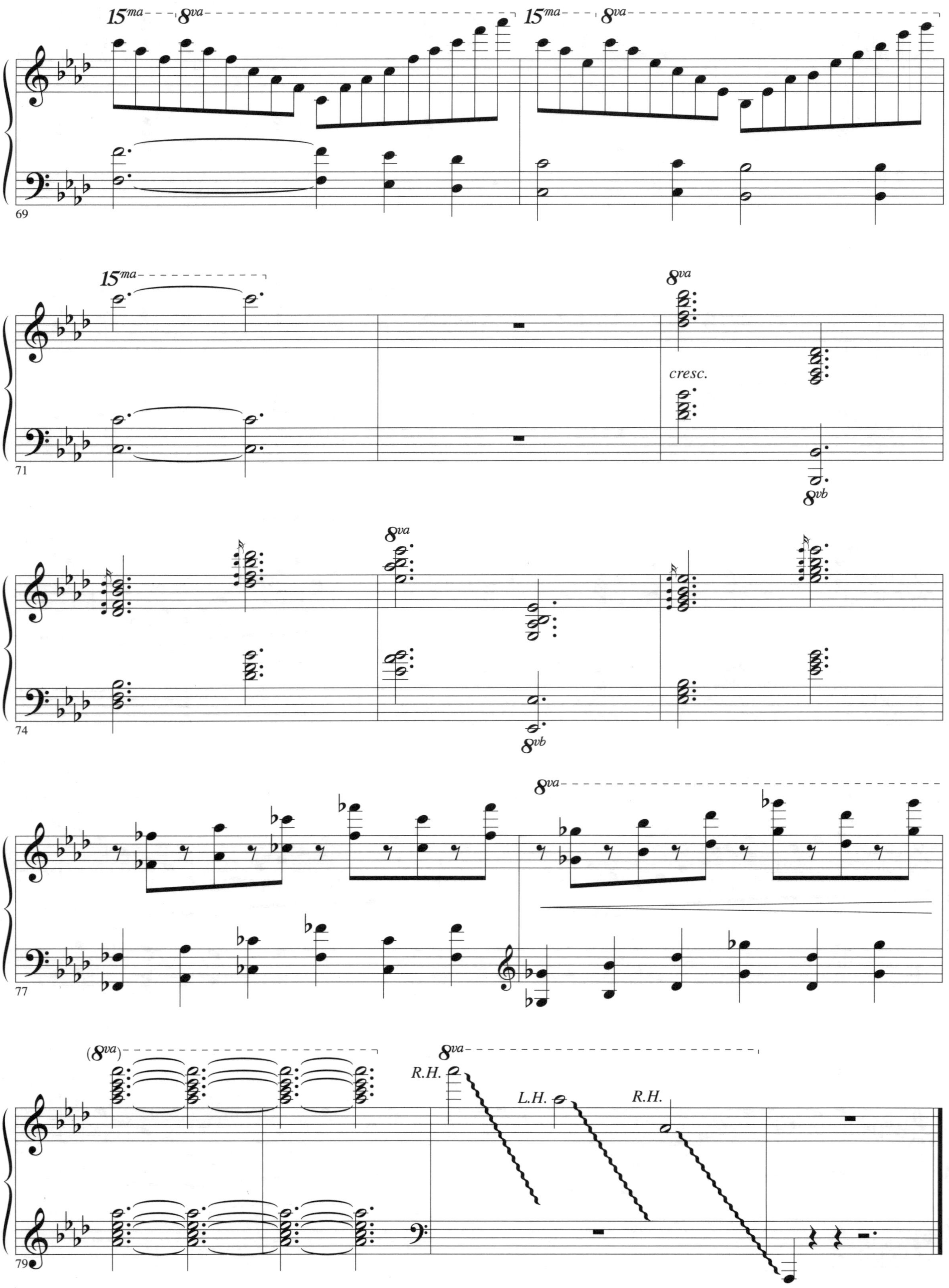
15ma
8va
69
71
cresc.
8vb
74
77
(8va)
R.H.
L.H.
79

You Are My All in All

(Solo Piano)

Words and Music by
DENNIS JERNIGAN
Arranged and orchestrated by Bruce Greer

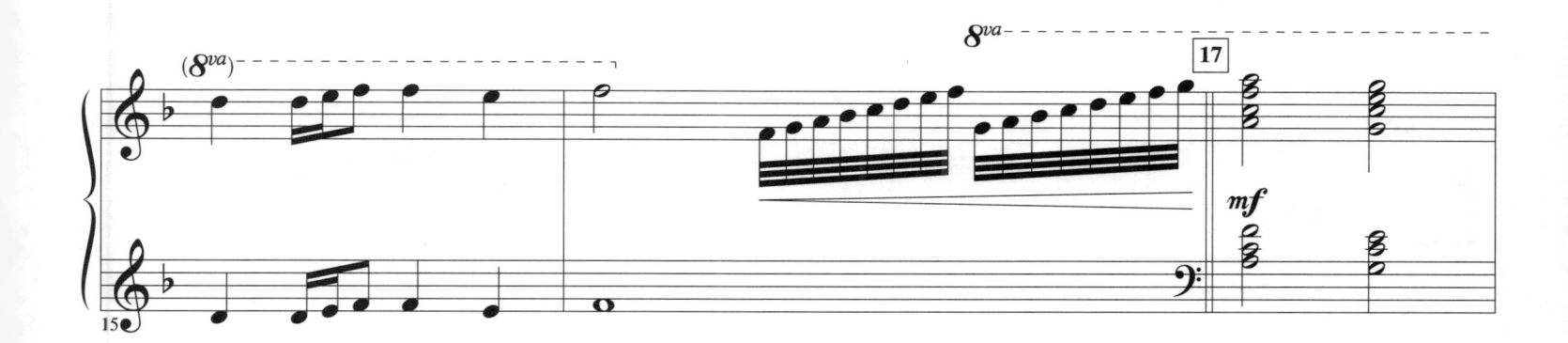

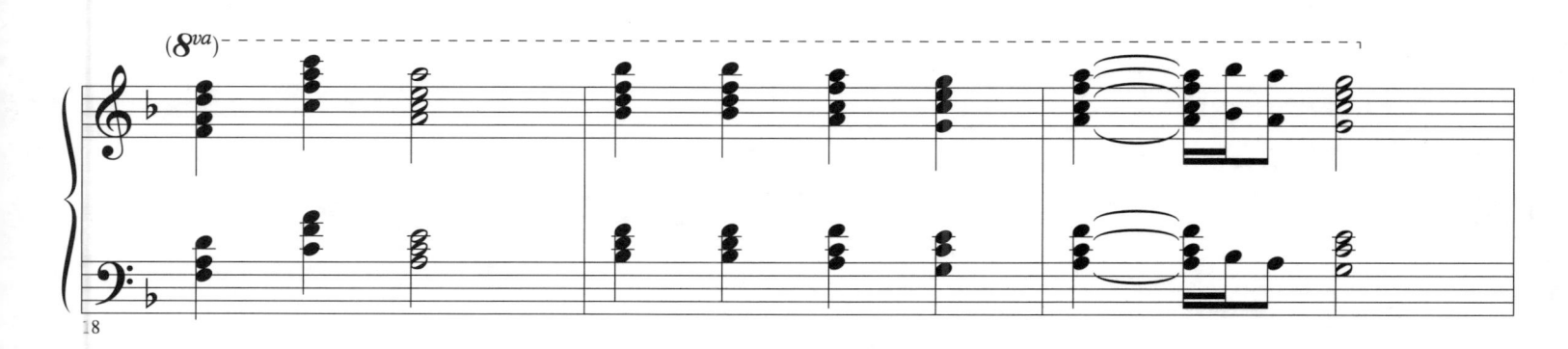

Gently (♩ = ca. 63)

© Copyright 1990 Shepherd's Heart Music, Inc. (admin. by Dayspring Music, Inc.)/BMI.
All Rights Reserved. Used by Permission.

EVEN IF YOU POSSESS A **CCLI** LICENSE YOU CANNOT COPY ANY MUSIC FROM THIS BOOK.
If you have questions about CCLI, please call 800 / 234-2446.

*NOTE: The R.H. arpeggios (bars 25-28) have been simplified from the actual recording to facilitate playing them against the L.H. melody.

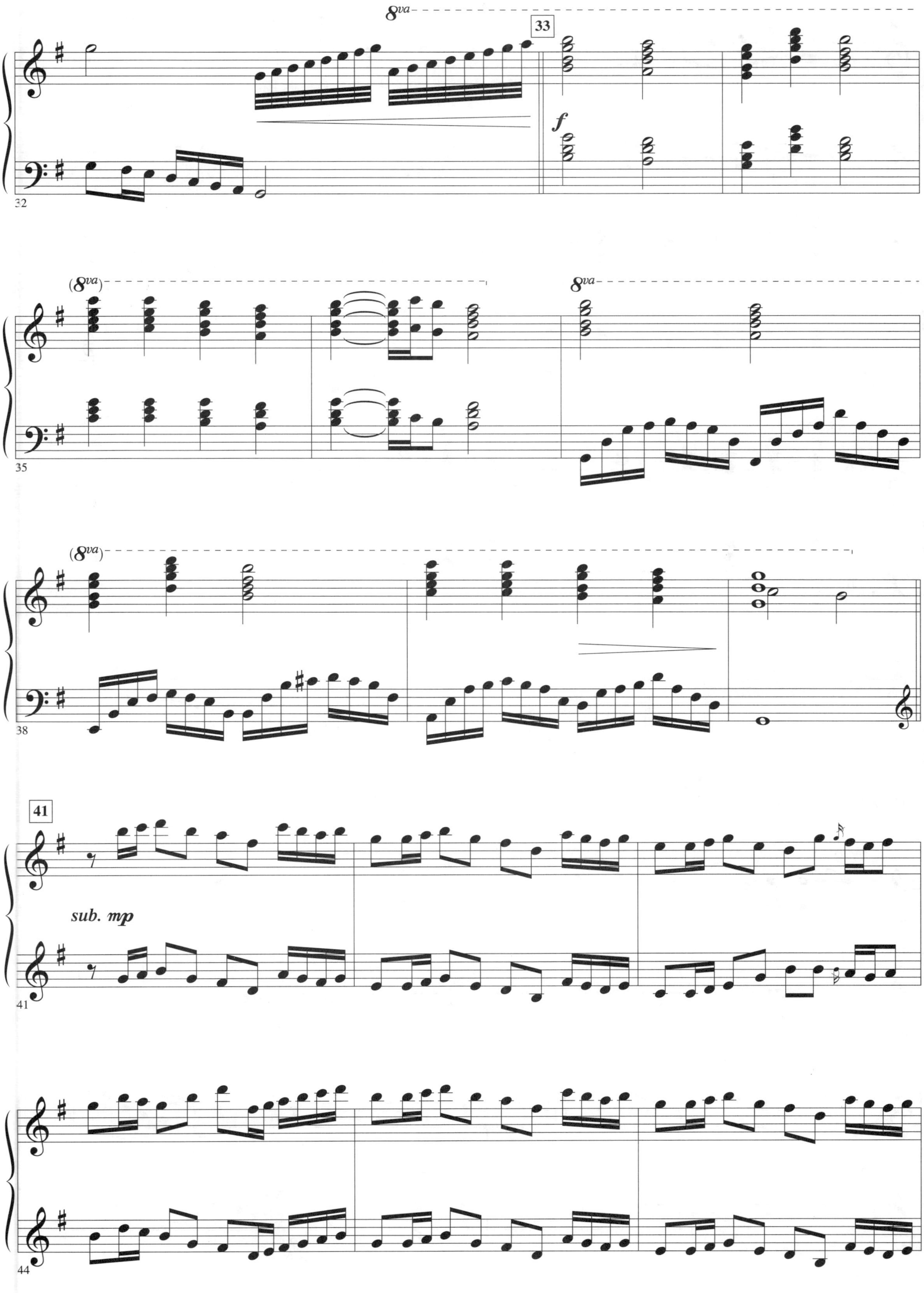
8va
33
f
32
(8va)
8va
35
(8va)
38
41
sub. mp
41
44

49
8va
f
47
(8va)
8va
51
(8va)
55
61
mp
8va
60
(8va)
64
8va
p
rit.
ad lib.
69
Ped.

He Is Our Peace

with It Is Well with My Soul

(Solo Piano)

Words and Music by
KANDELA GROVES
Arranged and orchestrated by Bruce Greer

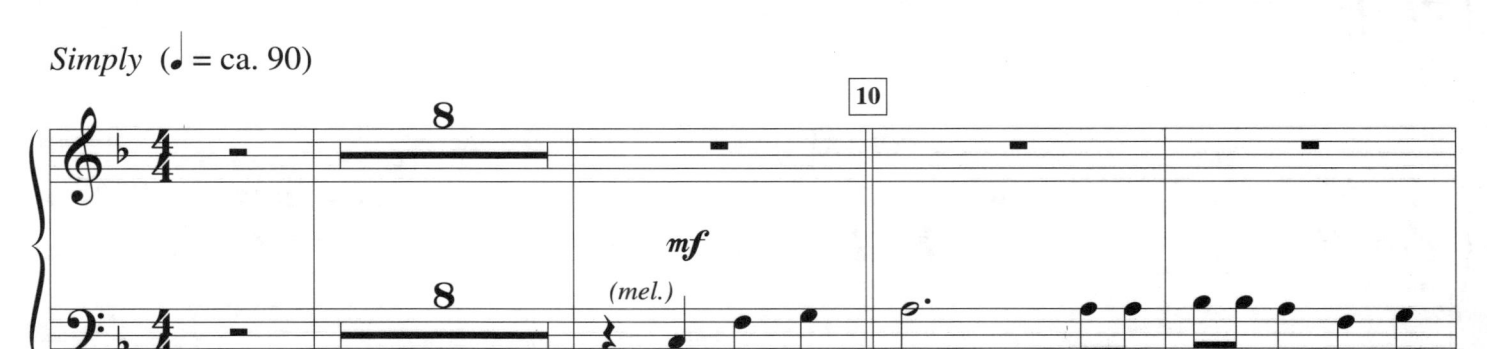

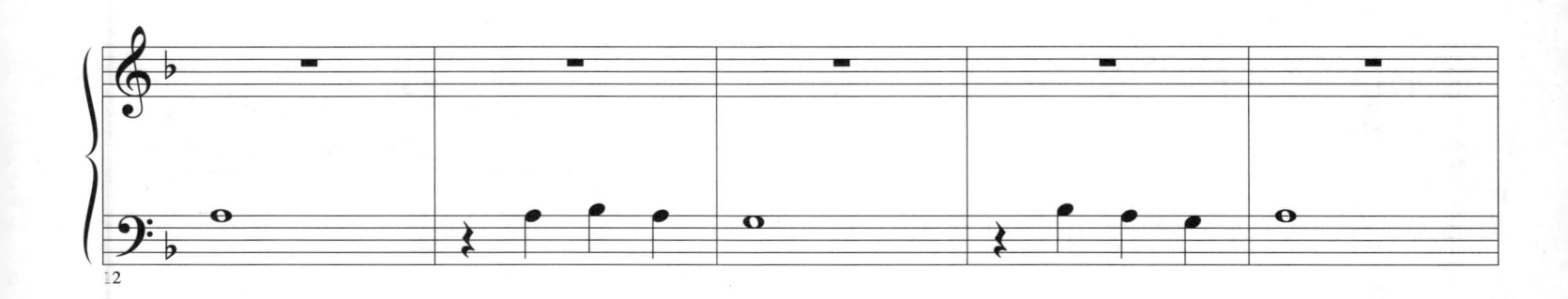

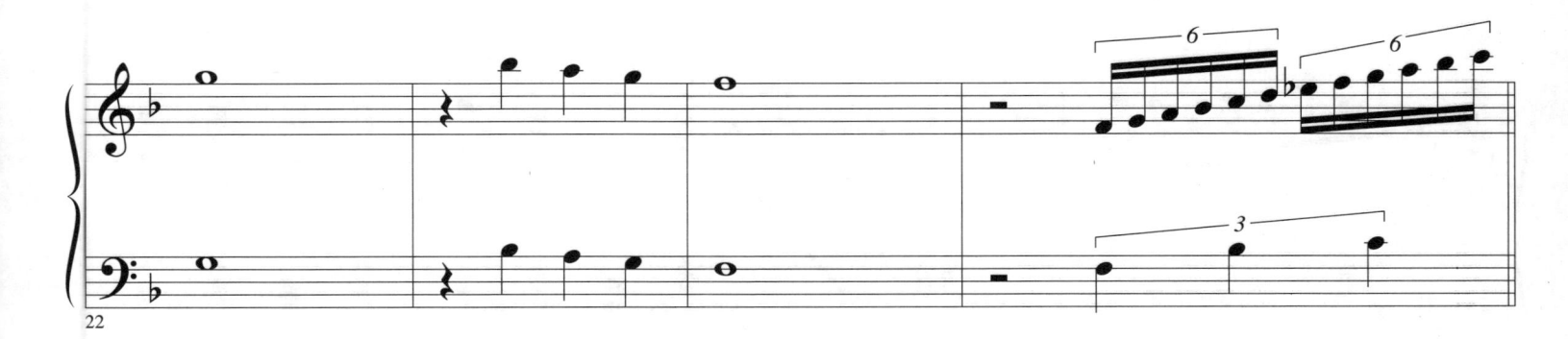

© Copyright 1975 Maranatha! Music (admin. The Copyright Co., Nashville, TN).
All Rights Reserved. Used by Permission.

EVEN IF YOU POSSESS A CCLI LICENSE YOU CANNOT COPY ANY MUSIC FROM THIS BOOK.
If you have questions about CCLI, please call 800 / 234-2446.

IT IS WELL WITH MY SOUL (Spafford/Bliss)

Arr. © Copyright 1995 Maranatha! Music (admin. The Copyright Co., Nashville, TN). All Rights Reserved. Used by Permission.

* SOLO PIANO only (to end)

Come Just as You Are

(Solo Piano)

Words and Music by
JOSEPH SABOLICK
Arranged and orchestrated by Bruce Greer

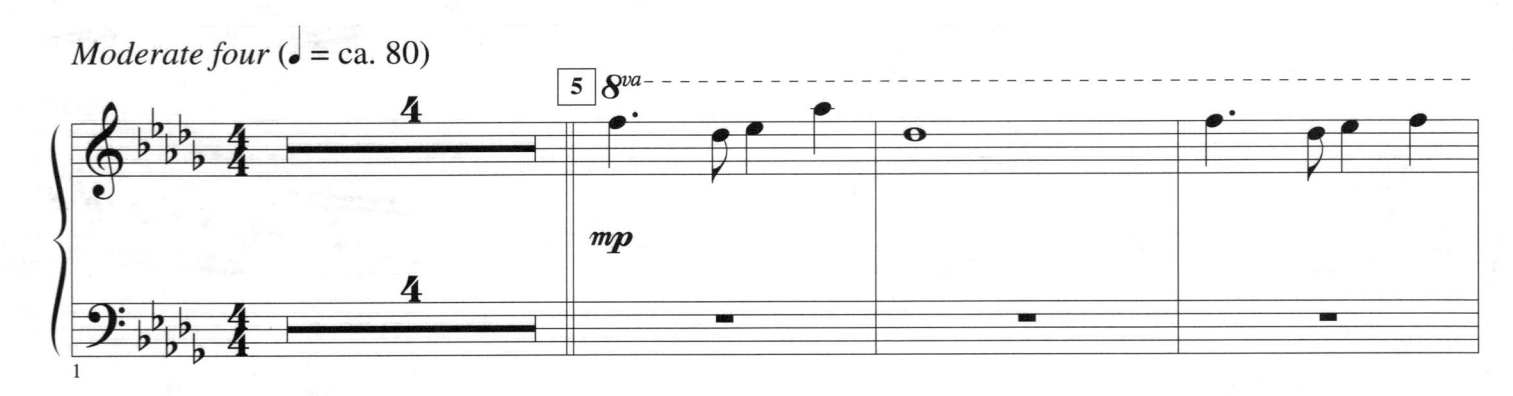

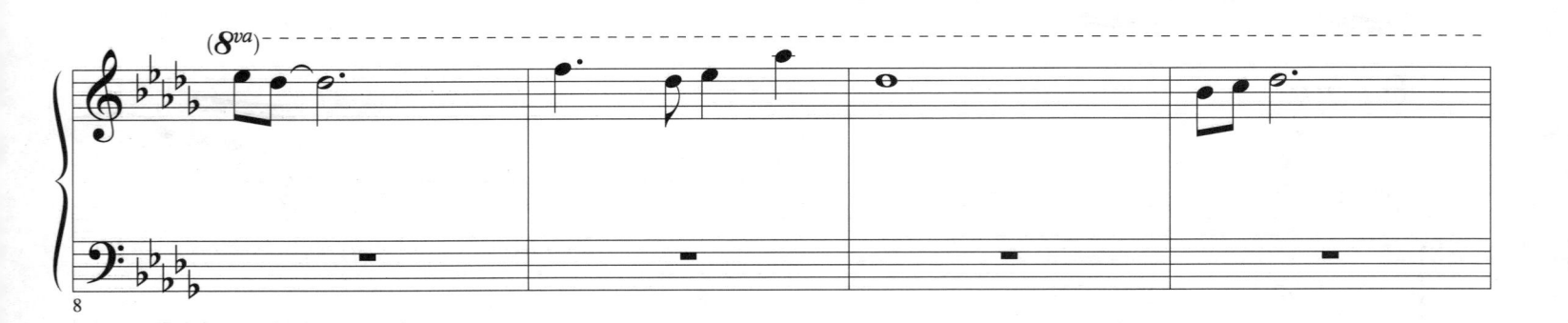

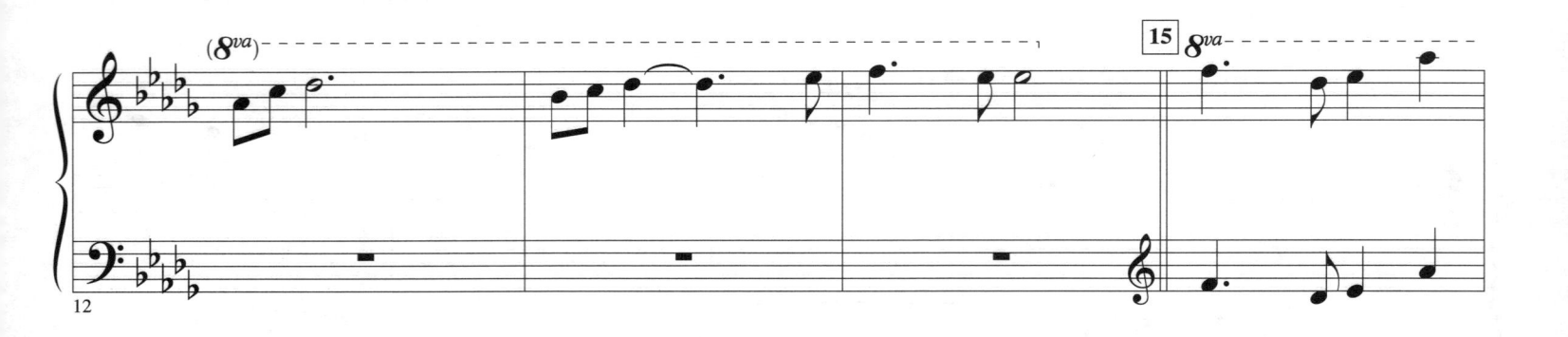

Moderate four (♩ = ca. 80)

© Copyright 1994 Maranatha Praise, Inc. (admin. The Copyright Co., Nashville, TN).
All Rights Reserved. Used by Permission.

EVEN IF YOU POSSESS A CCLI LICENSE YOU CANNOT COPY ANY MUSIC FROM THIS BOOK.
If you have questions about CCLI, please call 800 / 234-2446.

51

52

53

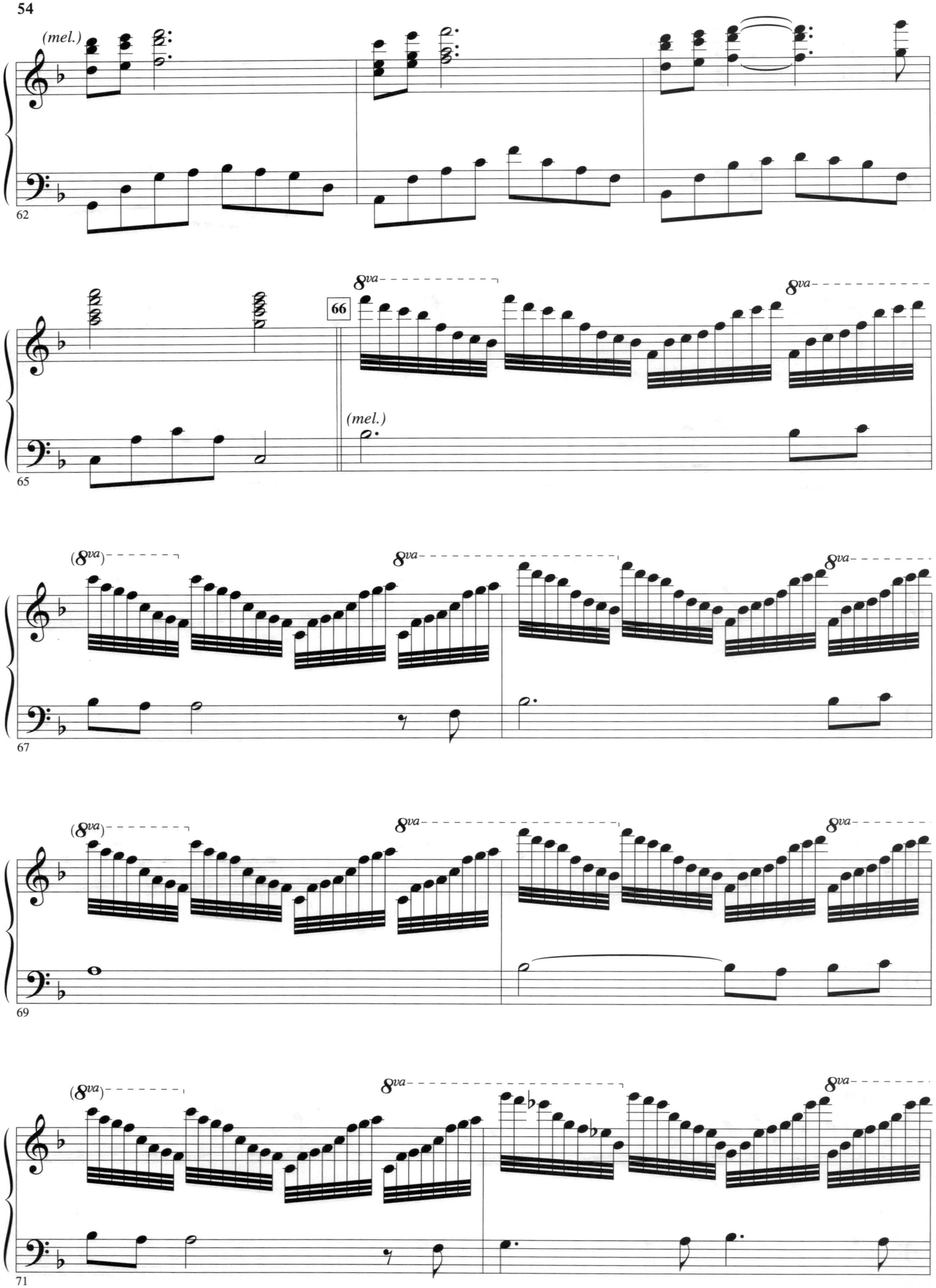
(mel.)
62
65
66
8va
(mel.)
67
(8va)
69
71

55

The optional *SECOND KEYBOARD* section of **I WILL CELEBRATE!** begins on the next page. Having these parts available gives you the added flexibility of using these arrangements as *KEYBOARD DUETS*… as well as performing with accompaniment trax.

I Will Celebrate

(Second Keyboard)

Words and Music by
RITA BALOCHE
Orchestrated by Richard Kingsmore
Arranged by Bruce Greer

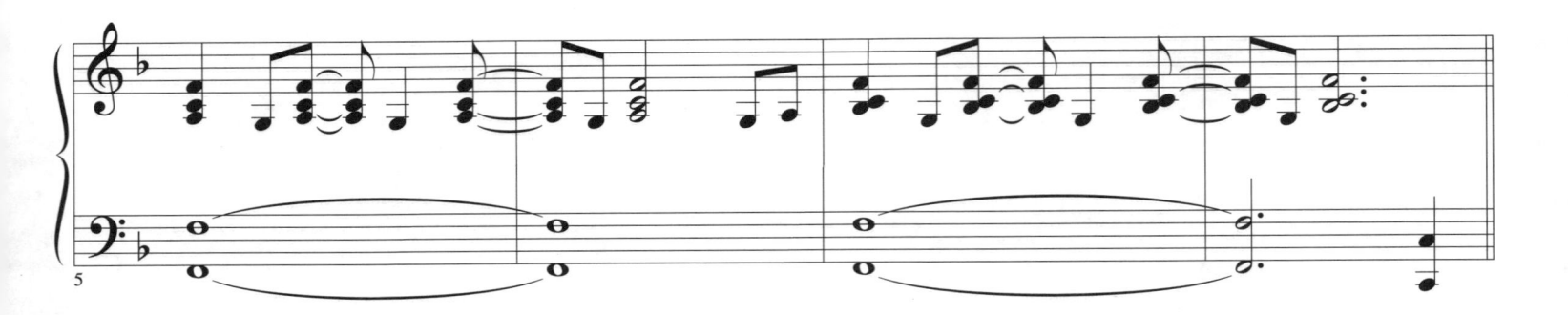

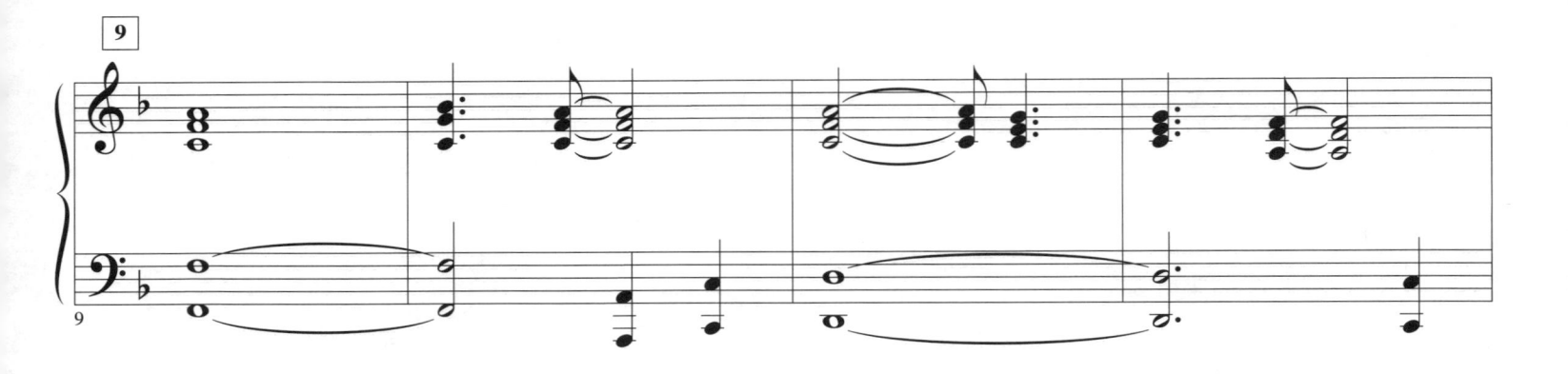

In two ($\d$ = ca. 84)

© Copyright 1990 Maranatha Praise, Inc. (admin. The Copyright Co., Nashville, TN).
All Rights Reserved. Used by Permission.

EVEN IF YOU POSSESS A CCLI LICENSE YOU CANNOT COPY ANY MUSIC FROM THIS BOOK.
If you have questions about CCLI, please call 800 / 234-2446.

25 *More movement*

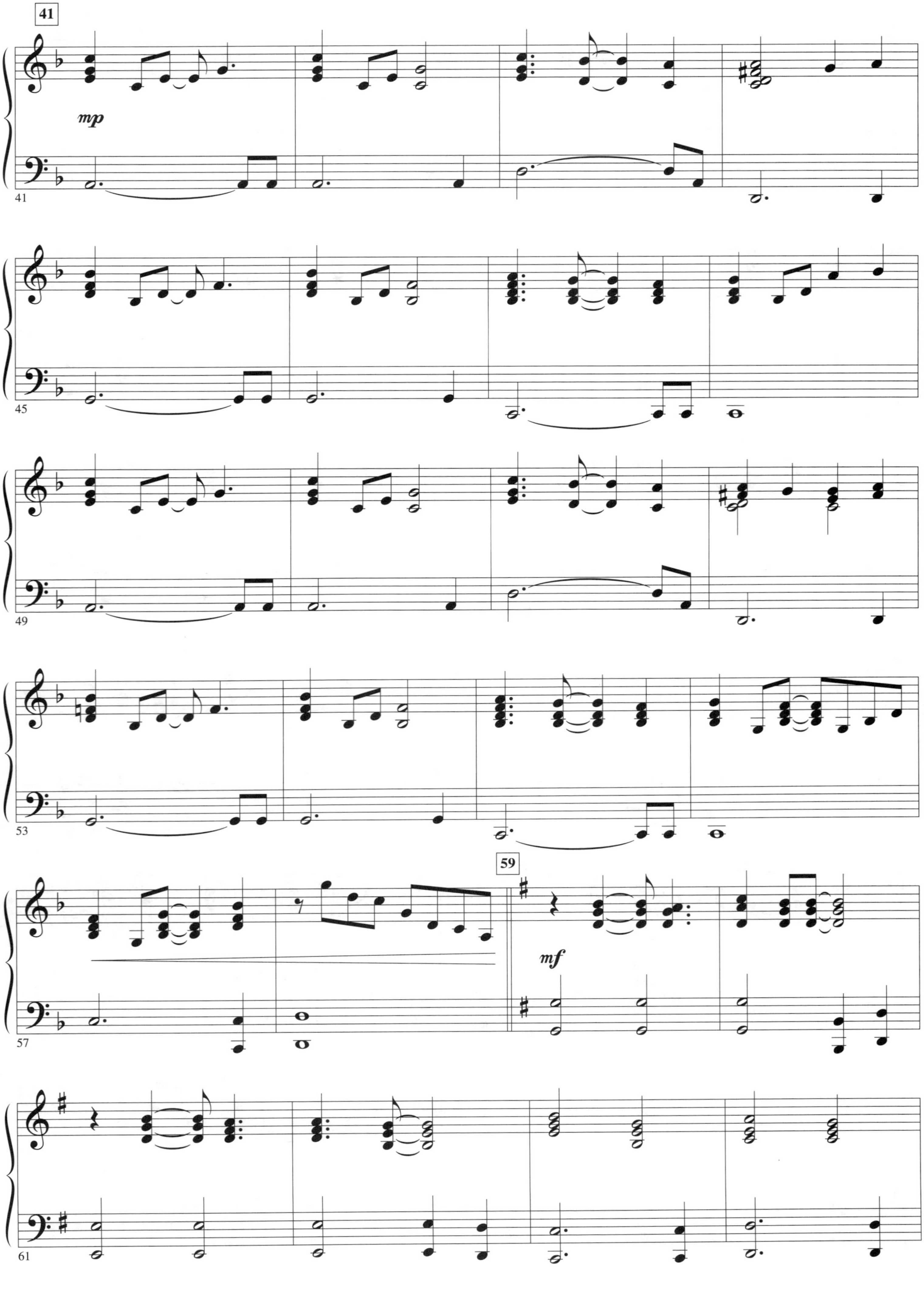
41
mp
41
45
49
53
59
mf
57
61

61

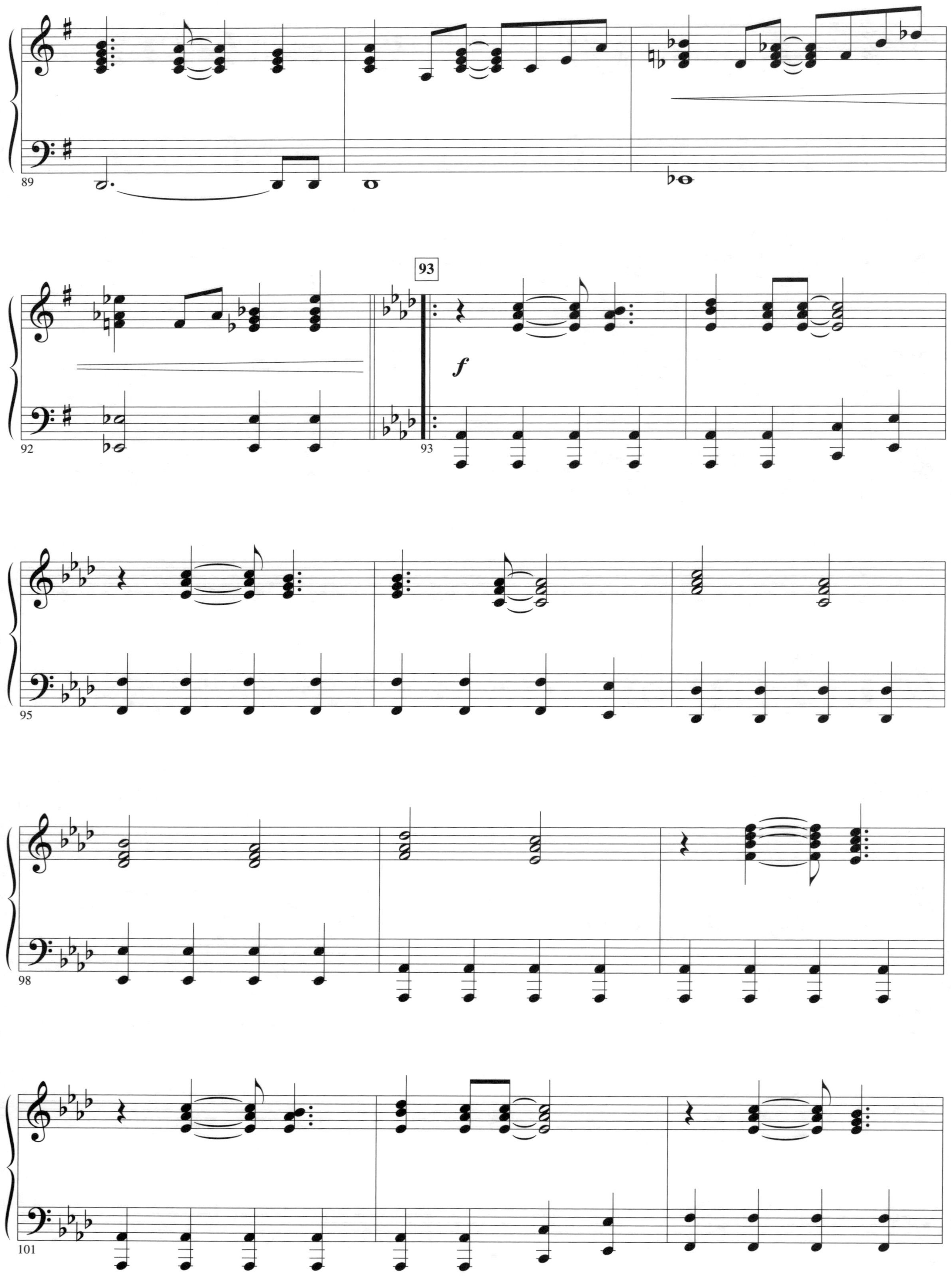
89
92
93
f
93
95
98
101

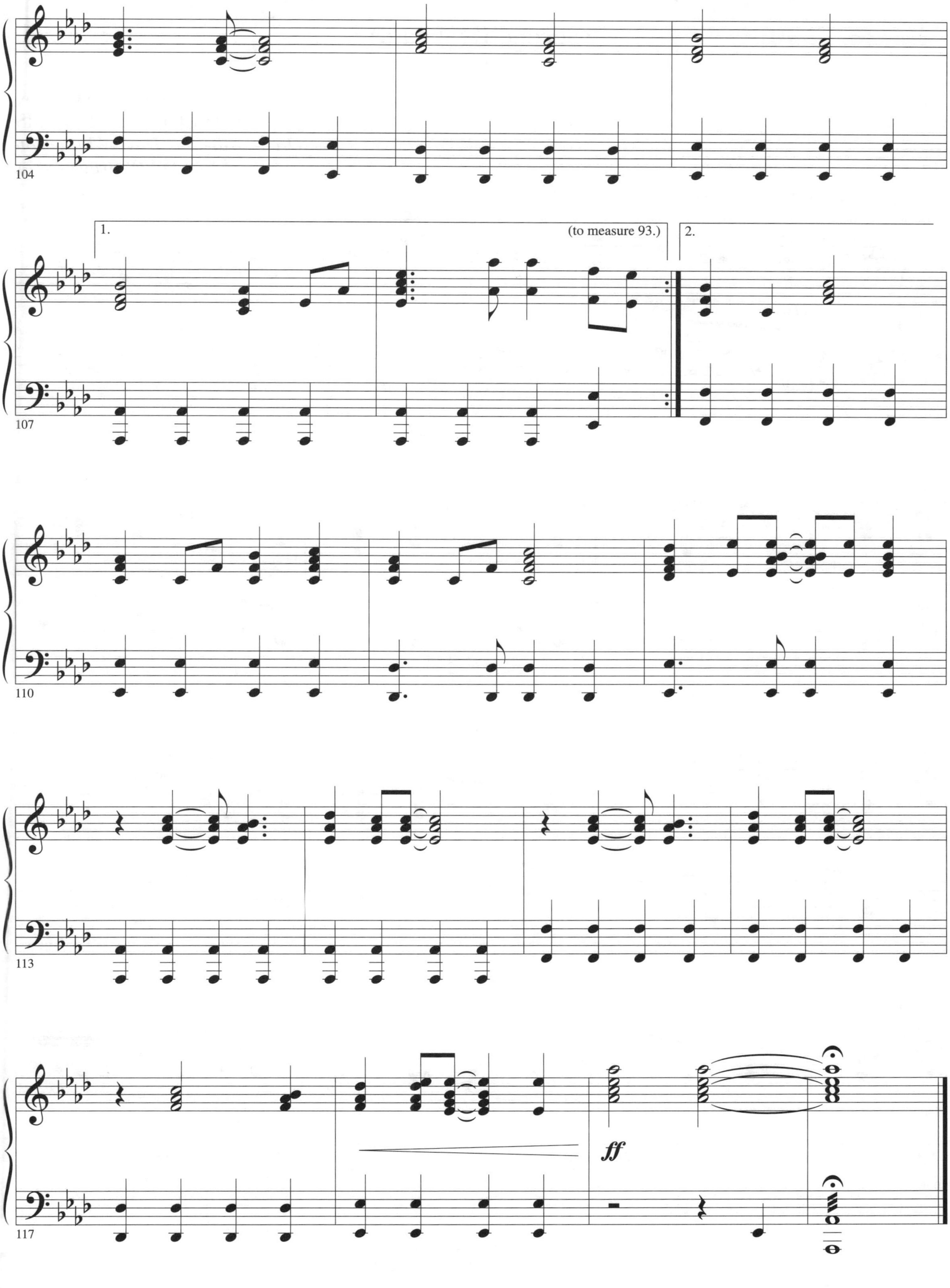
104
1.
(to measure 93.)
2.
107
110
113
117
ff

We Declare Your Majesty

(Second Keyboard)

Words and Music by
MALCOLM DU PLESSIS
Orchestrated by Dave Williamson
Arranged by Bruce Greer

Expressively ($\quarternote$ = ca. 66)

© Copyright 1985 Maranatha Praise, Inc. (admin. The Copyright Co., Nashville, TN) Except ThankYou Music for Europe.
All Rights Reserved. Used by Permission.

EVEN IF YOU POSSESS A **CCLI** LICENSE YOU CANNOT COPY ANY MUSIC FROM THIS BOOK.
If you have questions about CCLI, please call 800 / 234-2446.

65

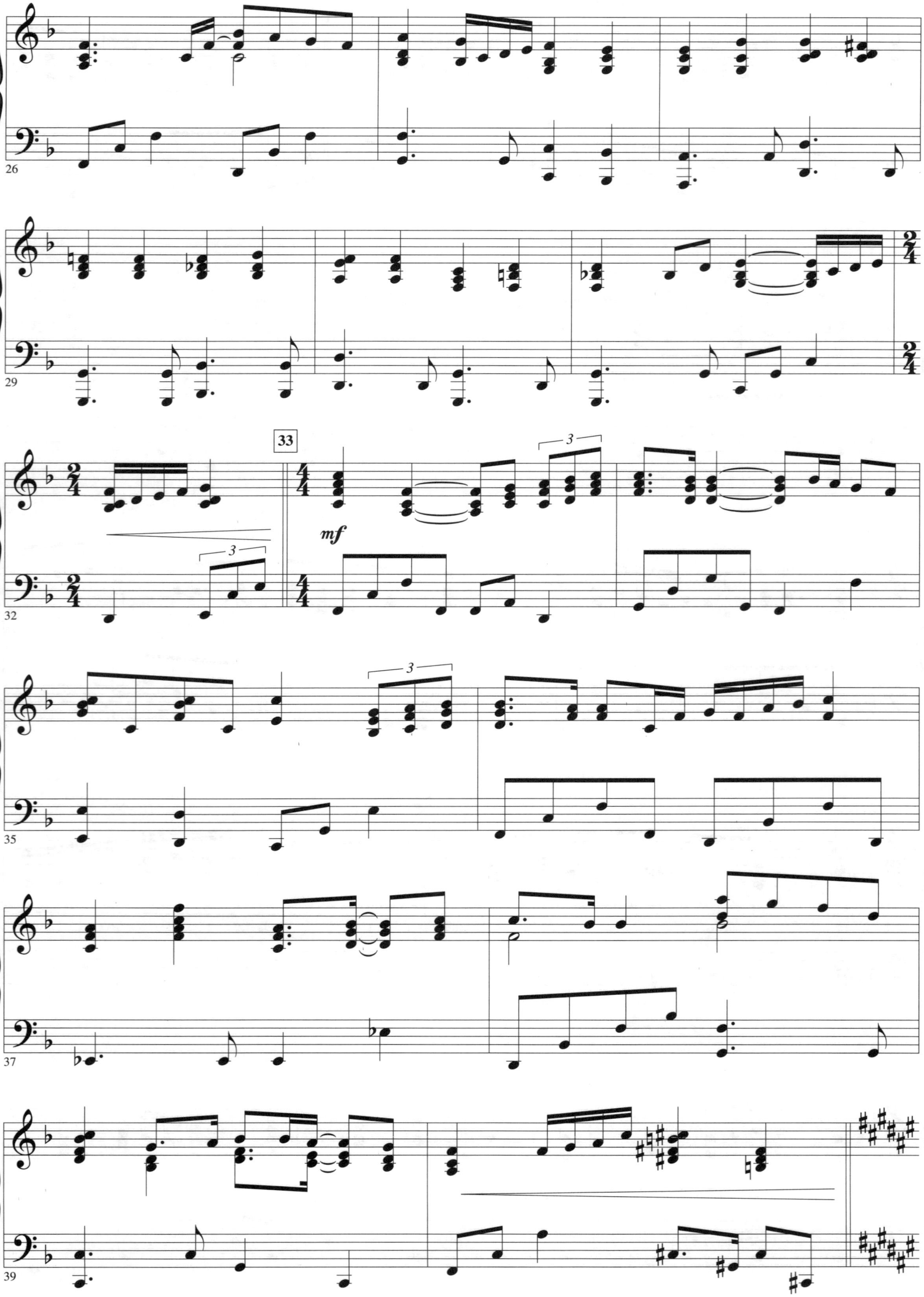
26
29
32
33
mf
3
35
37
39

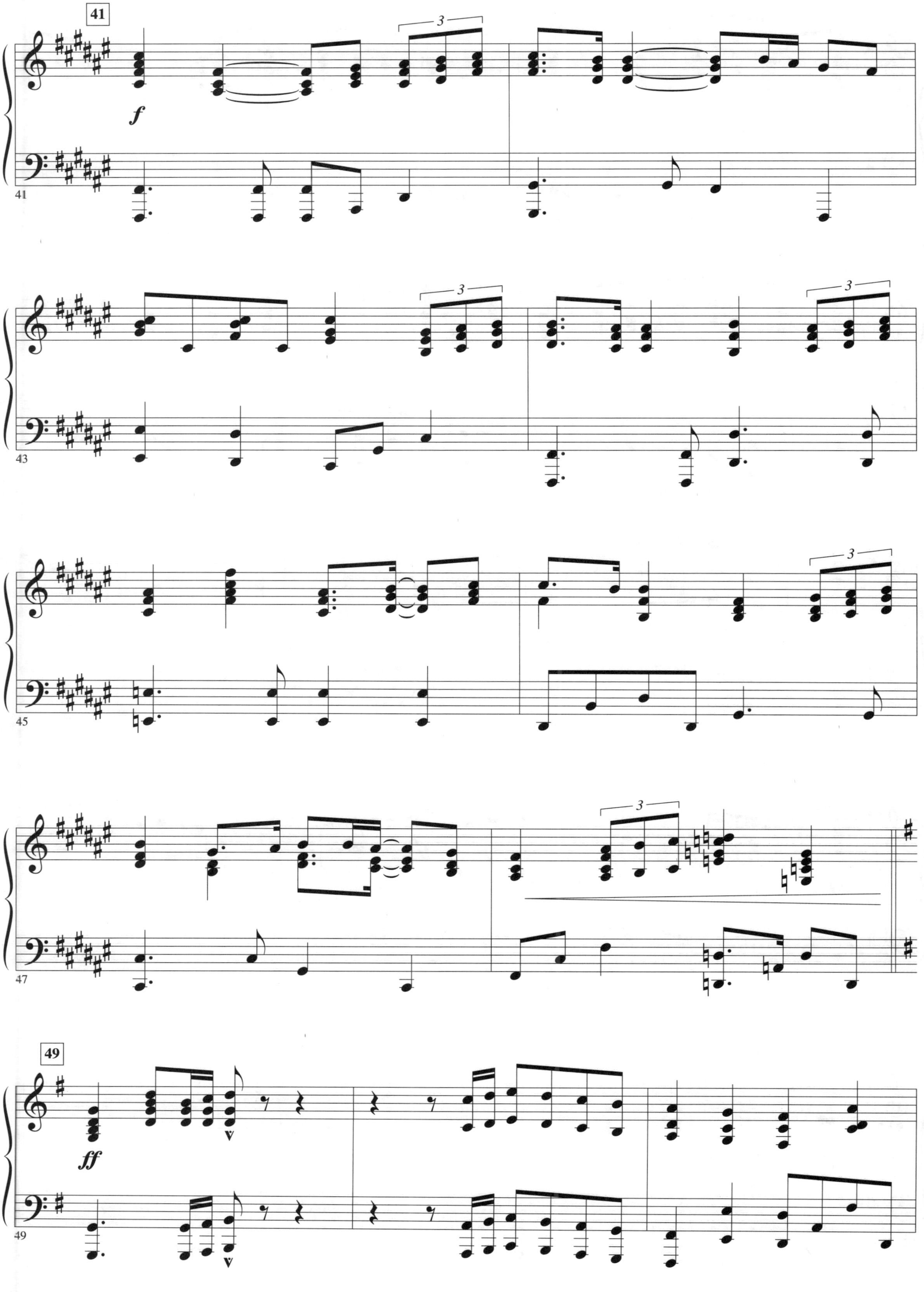
41
f
41
43
45
47
49
ff
49

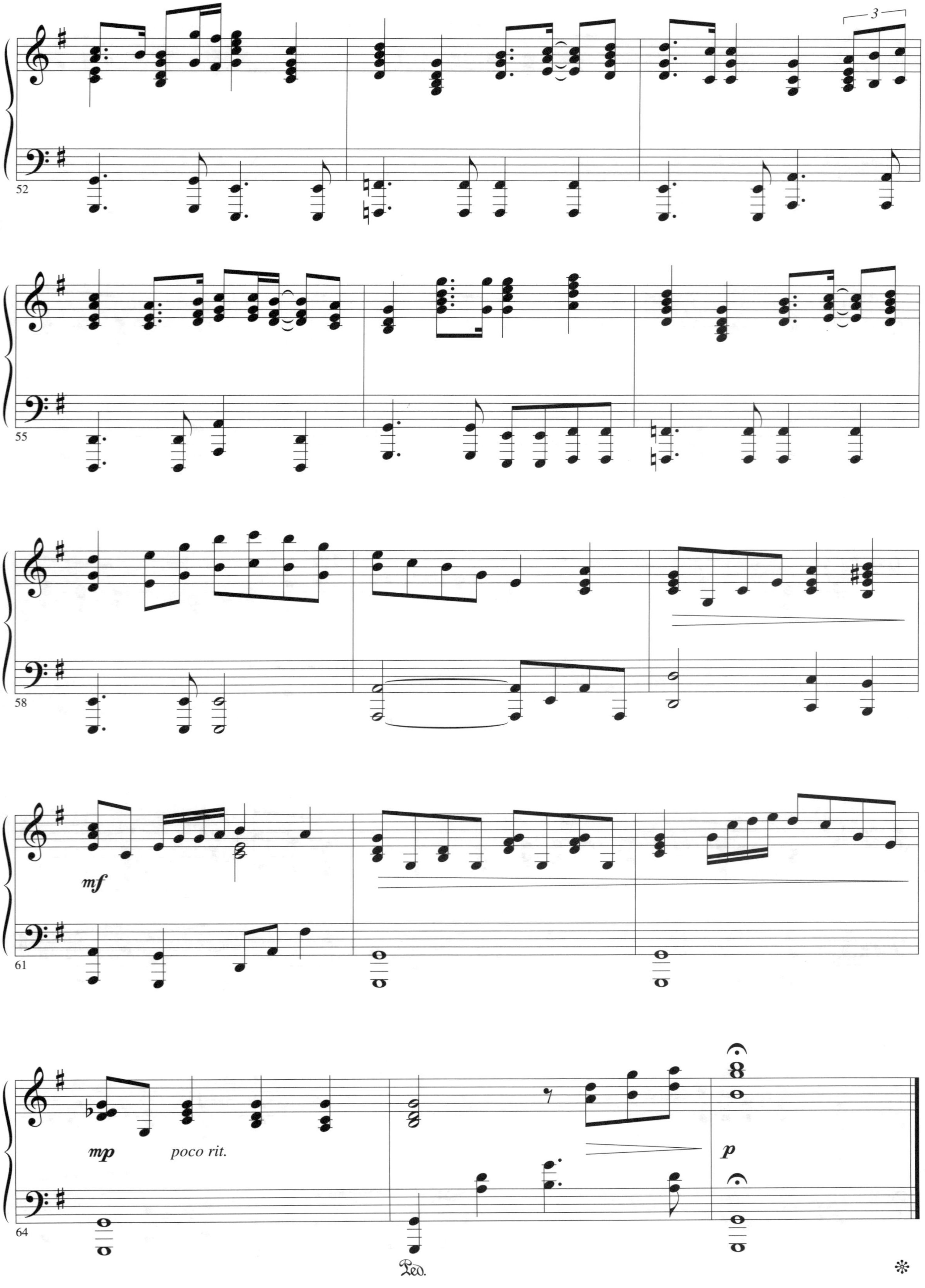
3
52
55
58
61
mf
64
mp
poco rit.
p
Ped.
*

Jesus, Draw Me Close
with I Am Thine, O Lord
(Second Keyboard)

Words and Music by
RICK FOUNDS
Track arranged by Gary Rhodes
Arranged and orchestrated by Bruce Greer

Tenderly (♩ = ca. 88)

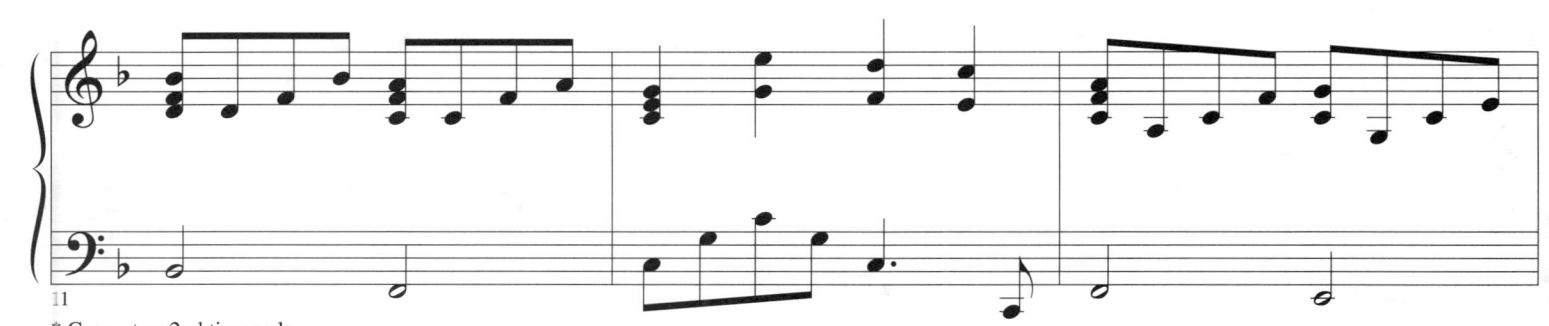

*Cue notes: 2nd time only

© Copyright 1990 Maranatha Praise, Inc. (admin. The Copyright Co., Nashville, TN).
All Rights Reserved. Used by Permission.

EVEN IF YOU POSSESS A CCLI LICENSE YOU CANNOT COPY ANY MUSIC FROM THIS BOOK.
If you have questions about CCLI, please call 800 / 234-2446.

I AM THINE, O LORD *(Crosby/Doane)*

Arr. © Copyright 1995 Word Music, Inc. All Rights Reserved.

71

54
57
mf
61
rit.
mf broadening
64 (JESUS, DRAW ME CLOSE)
f a tempo
64
67
70

(I AM THINE, O LORD)

89
mf poco rall.
92
Slightly slower
96
mp
Slowing
a tempo
100
poco rit.
104
rit.
p
107

Lord, I Lift Your Name on High
with All Hail the Power of Jesus' Name
(Second Keyboard)

Words and Music by
RICK FOUNDS
Arranged and orchestrated by Bruce Greer

Majestically ($\quarter = $ ca. 108)

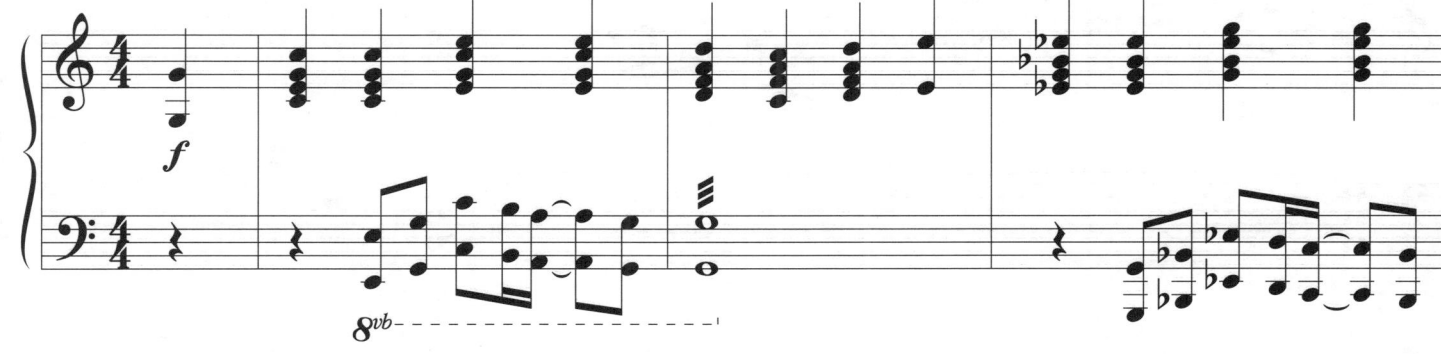

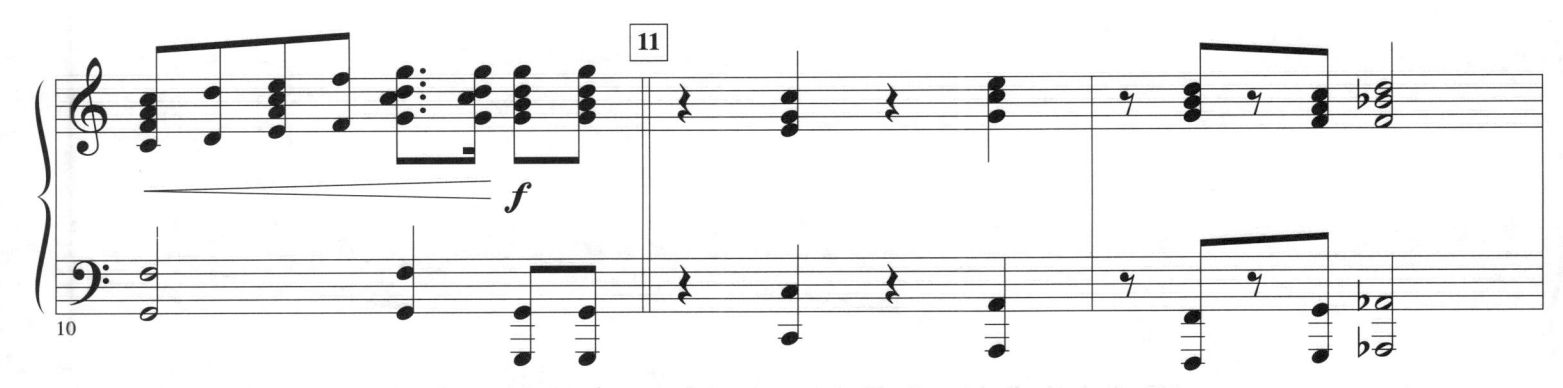

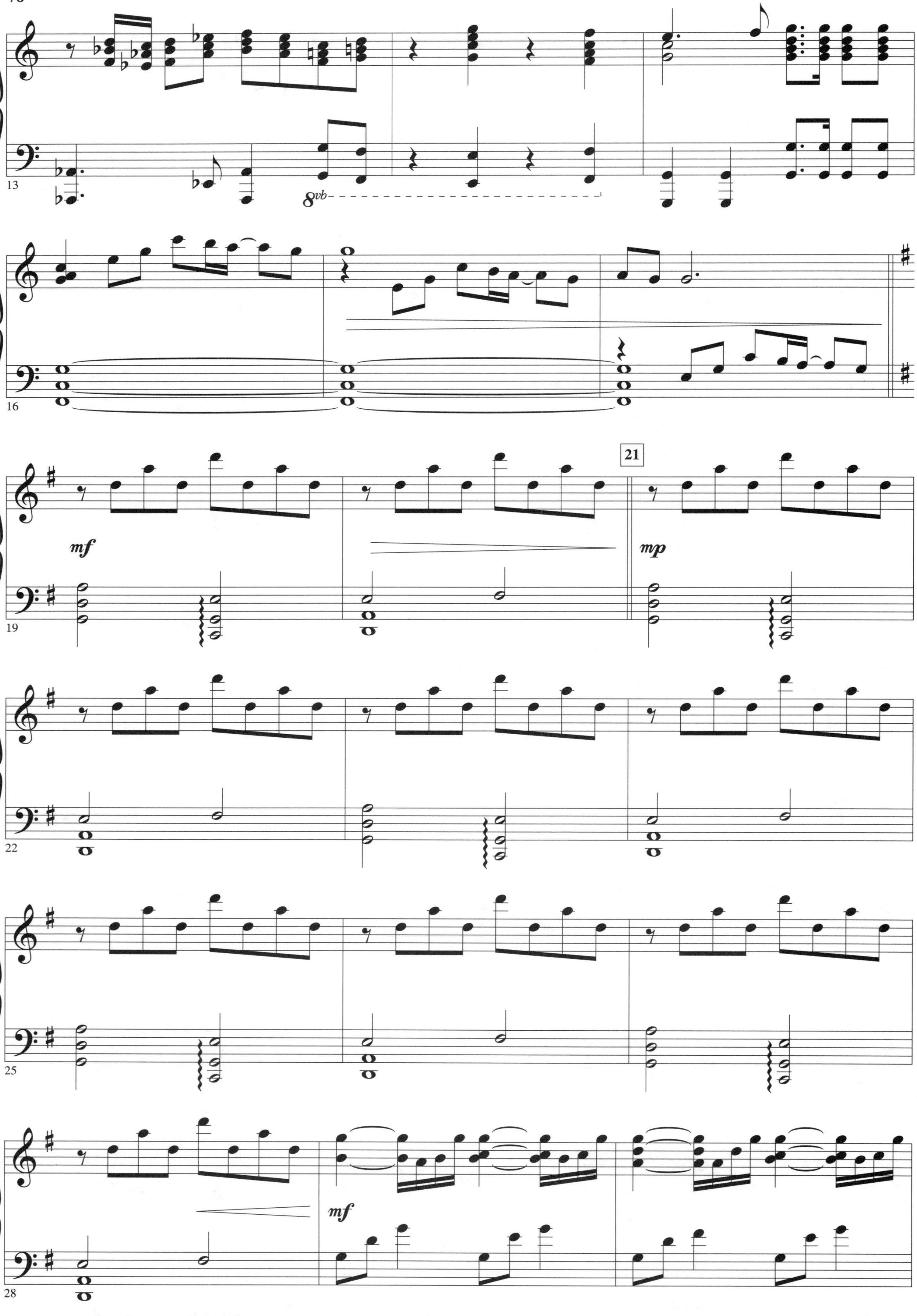
13
8vb
16
19
mf
21
mp
22
25
28
mf

77

ALL HAIL THE POWER OF JESUS' NAME *(Perronet/Holden)*

Arr. © Copyright 1995 Maranatha! Music (admin. The Copyright Co., Nashville, TN). All Rights Reserved. Used by Permission.

56 (LORD, I LIFT YOUR NAME ON HIGH)

65 (ALL HAIL THE POWER OF JESUS' NAME)

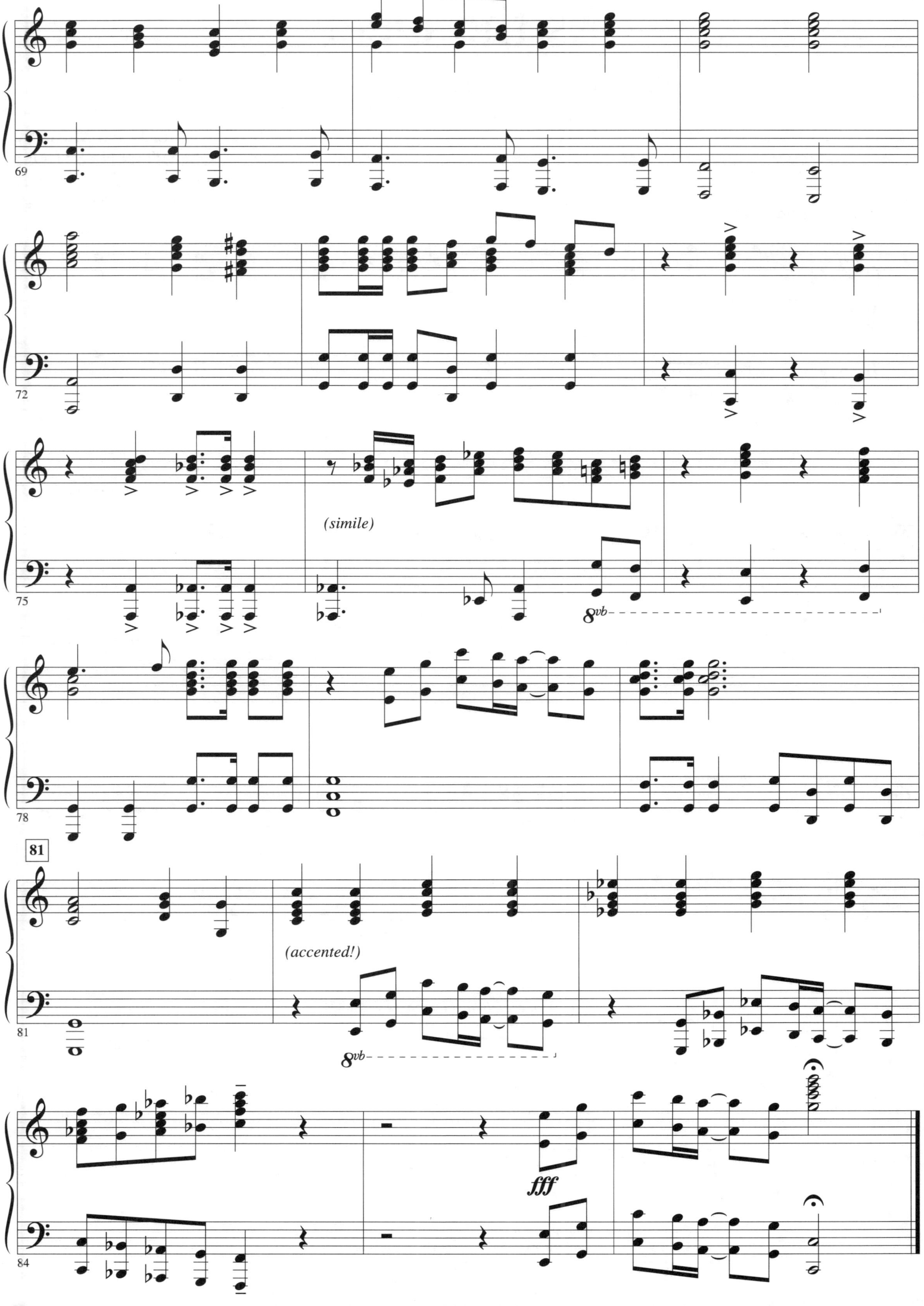
69
72
75
(simile)
8vb
78
81
(accented!)
8vb
84
fff

As the Deer
with Open Our Eyes, Lord
(Second Keyboard)

Words and Music by
MARTIN NYSTROM
Orchestrated by Don Hart
Arranged by Bruce Greer

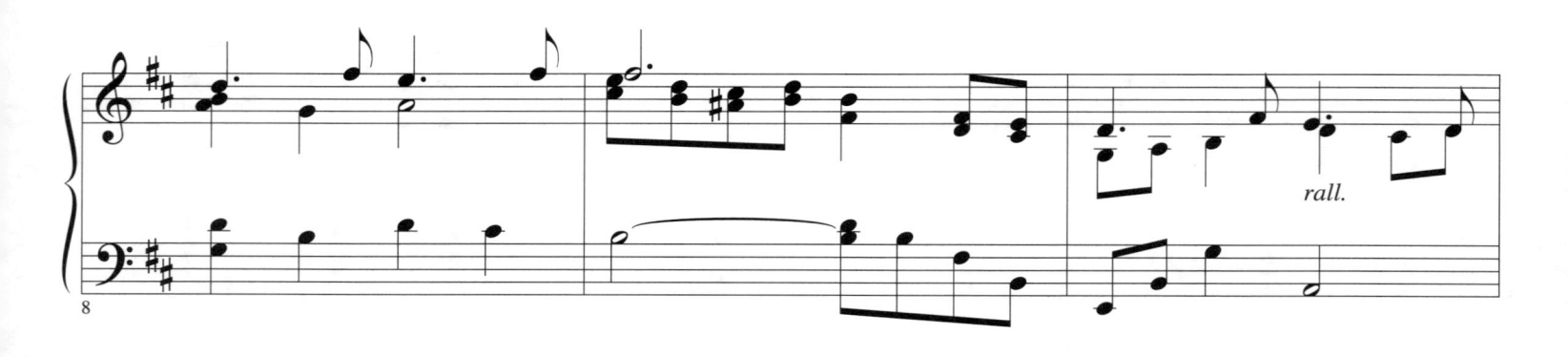

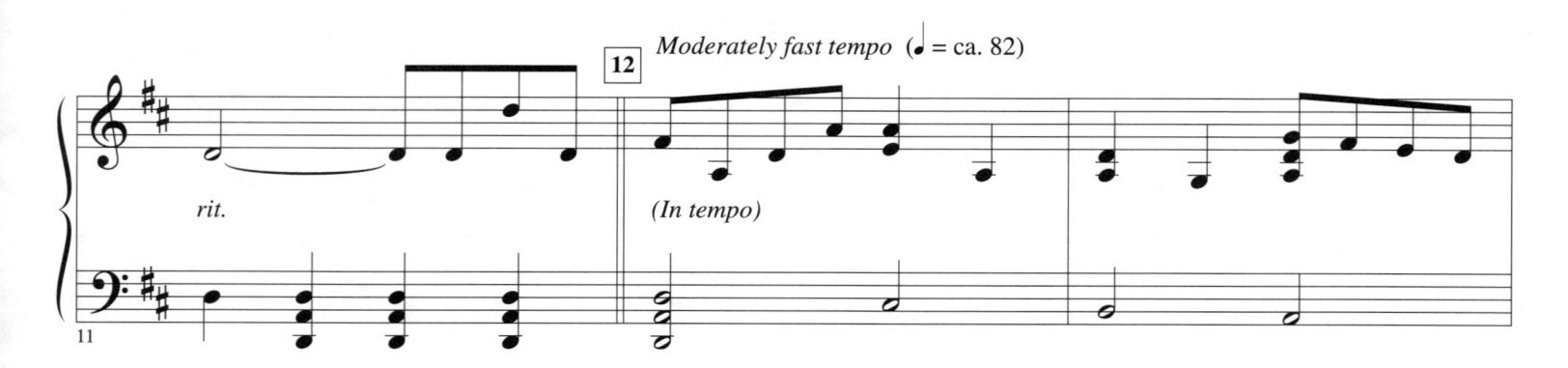

Slowly and freely

© Copyright 1984 Maranatha Praise, Inc. (admin. The Copyright Co., Nashville, TN).
All Rights Reserved. Used by Permission.

EVEN IF YOU POSSESS A **CCLI** LICENSE YOU CANNOT COPY ANY MUSIC FROM THIS BOOK.
If you have questions about CCLI, please call 800 / 234-2446.

81

OPEN OUR EYES, LORD *(Robert Cull)*

Moderately fast tempo ($\quarternote$ = ca. 93)

© Copyright 1976 Maranatha Music (admin. The Copyright Co., Nashville, TN). All Rights Reserved. Used by Permission.

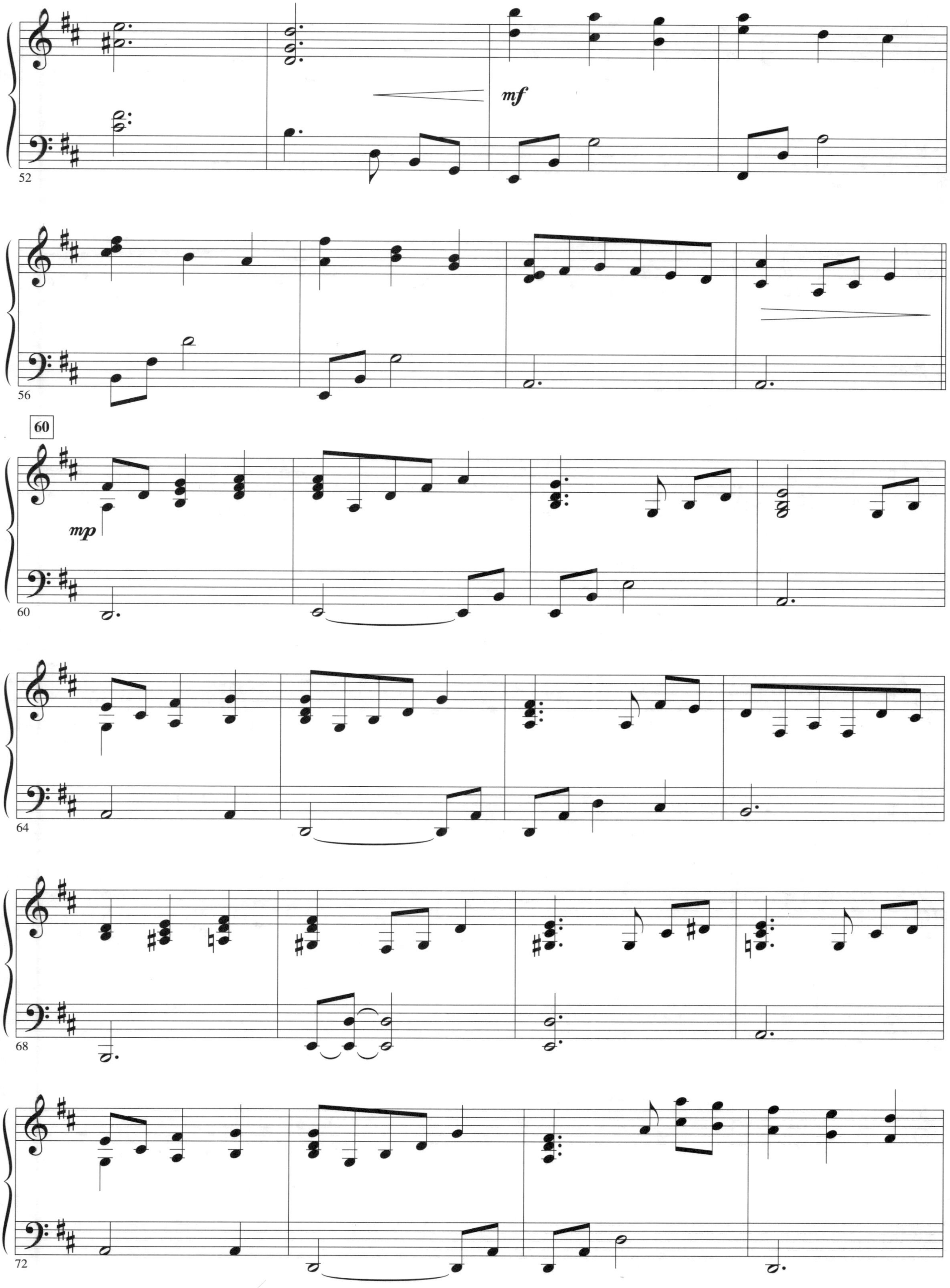
mf
52
56
60
mp
60
64
68
72

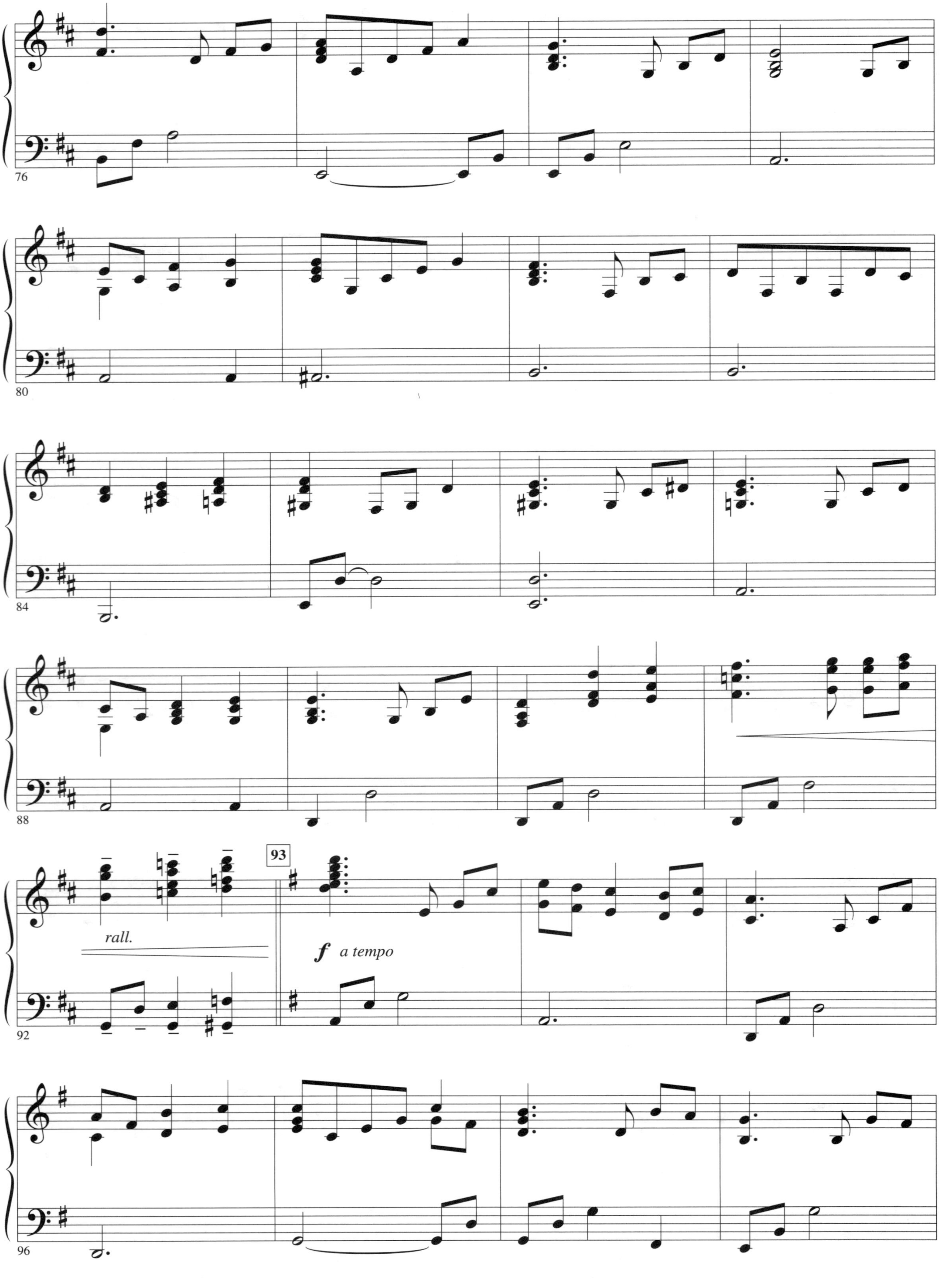
76
80
84
88
92
rall.
93
f a tempo
96

85

(AS THE DEER) *Broadly* (♩ = ca. 74)

You're Worthy of My Praise

(Second Keyboard)

Words and Music by
DAVID RUIS
Orchestrated by Don Hart
Arranged by Bruce Greer

Steady four (♩ = ca. 91)

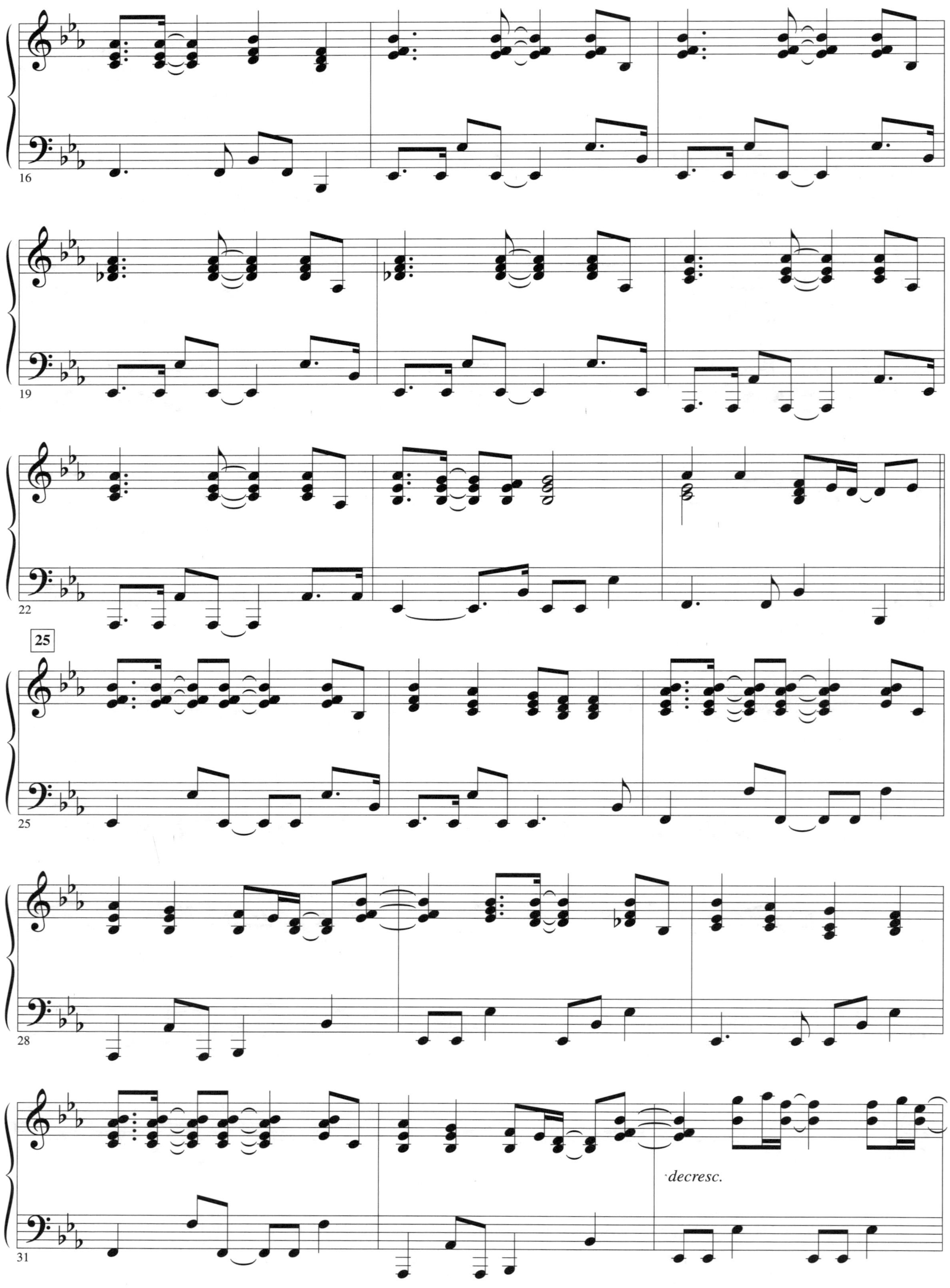
16
19
22
25
25
28
31
decresc.

89

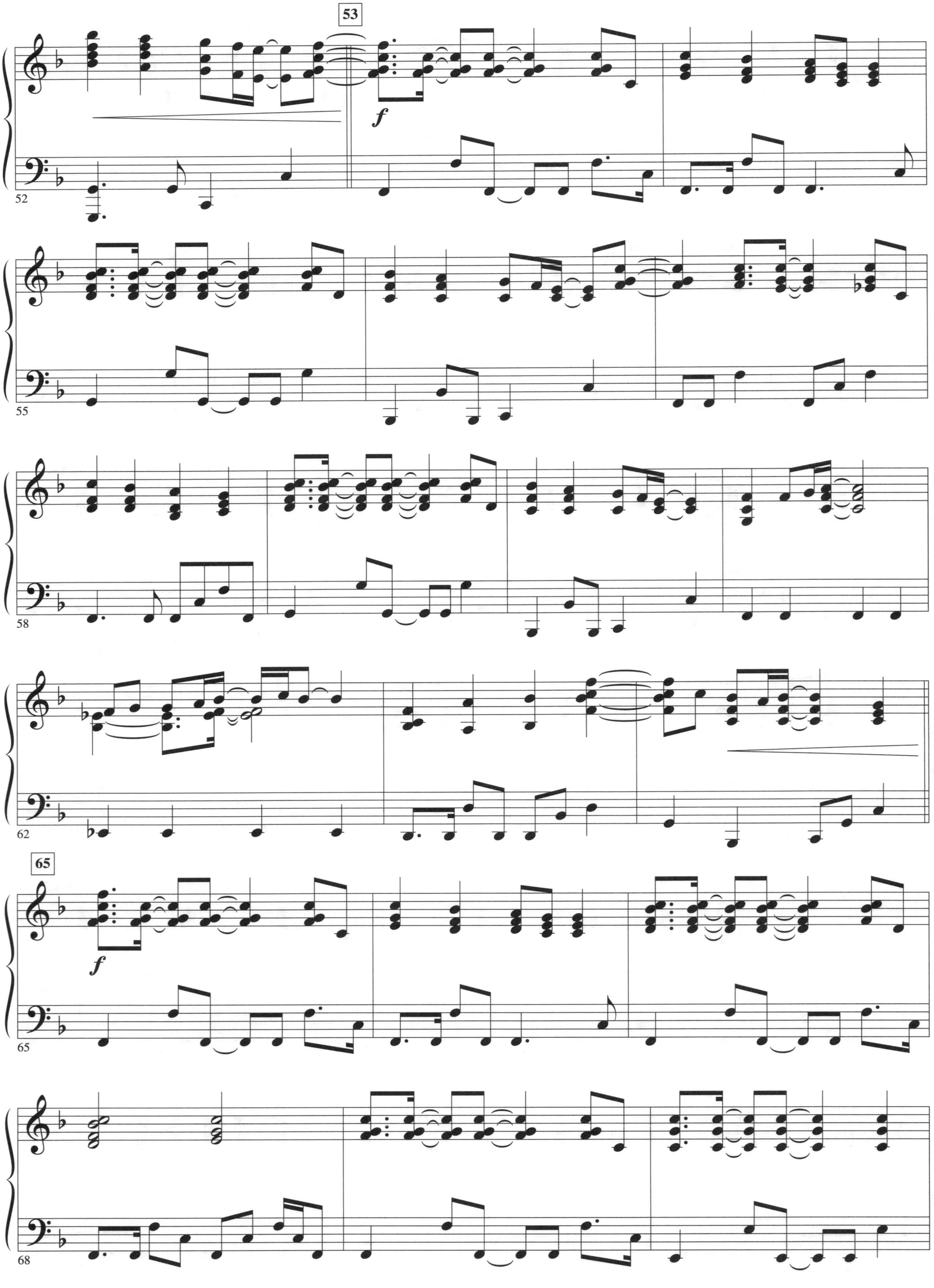
53
f
52
55
58
62
65
f
65
68

91

Behold, What Manner of Love
with O How I Love Jesus
(Second Keyboard)

Words and Music by
PATRICIA VAN TINE
Orchestrated and arranged by Bruce Greer

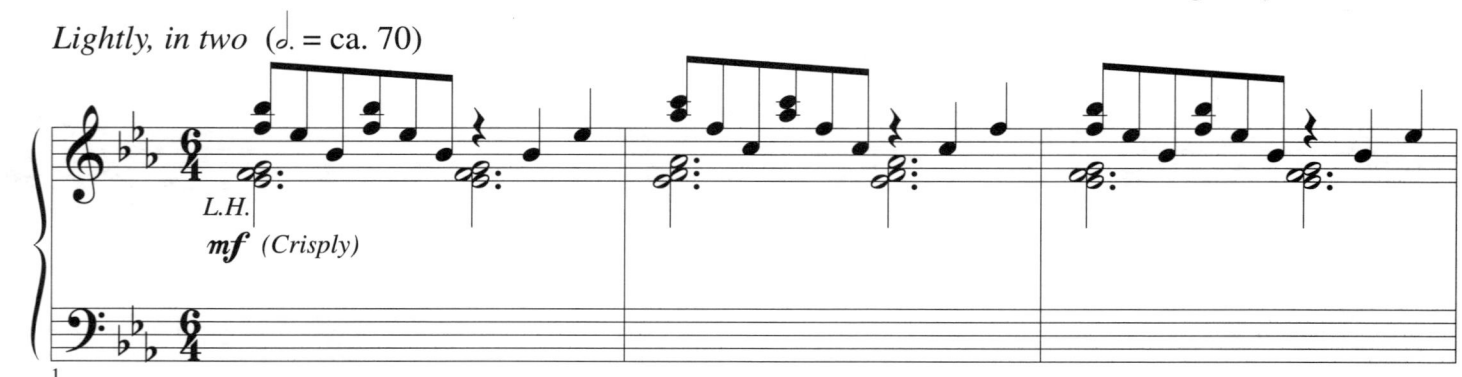

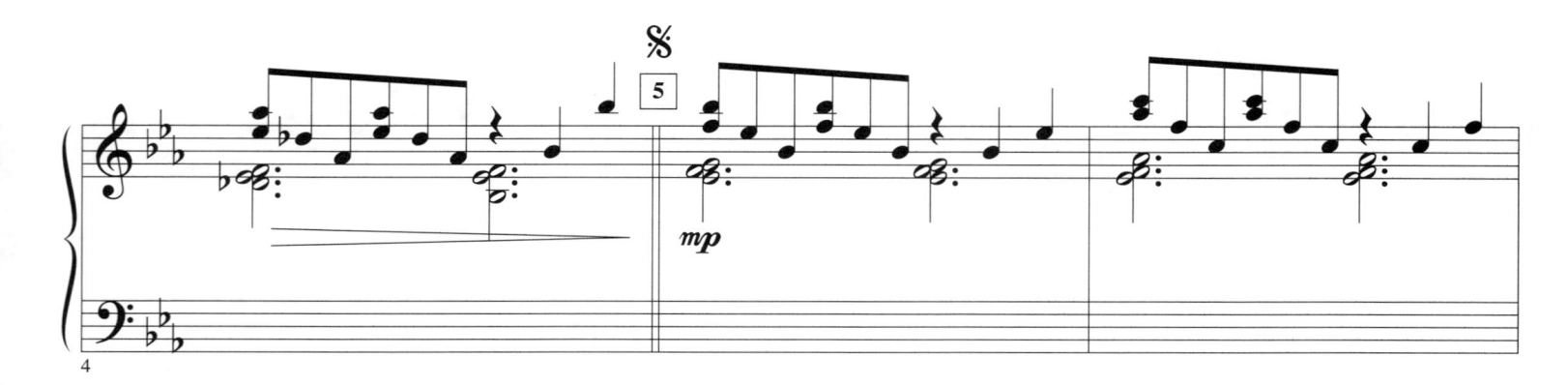

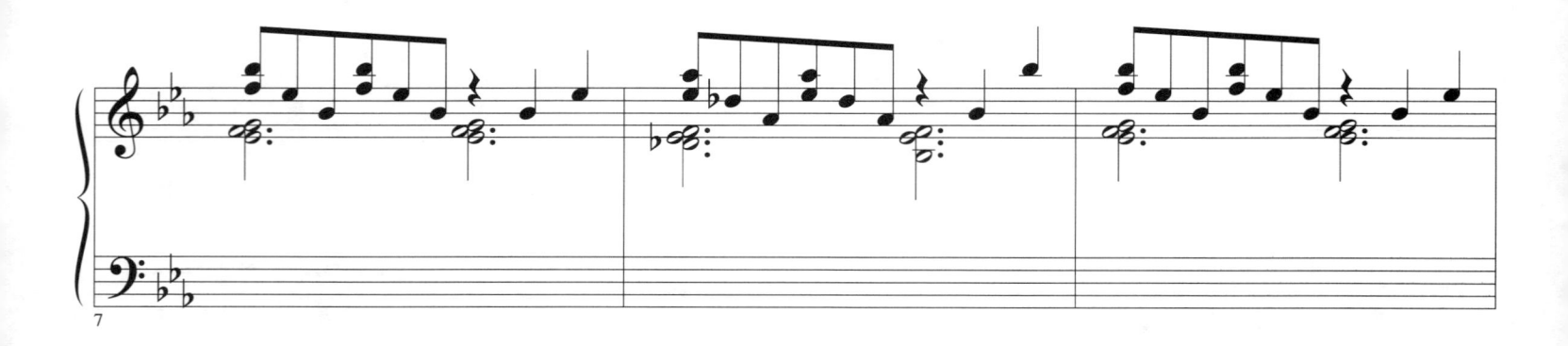

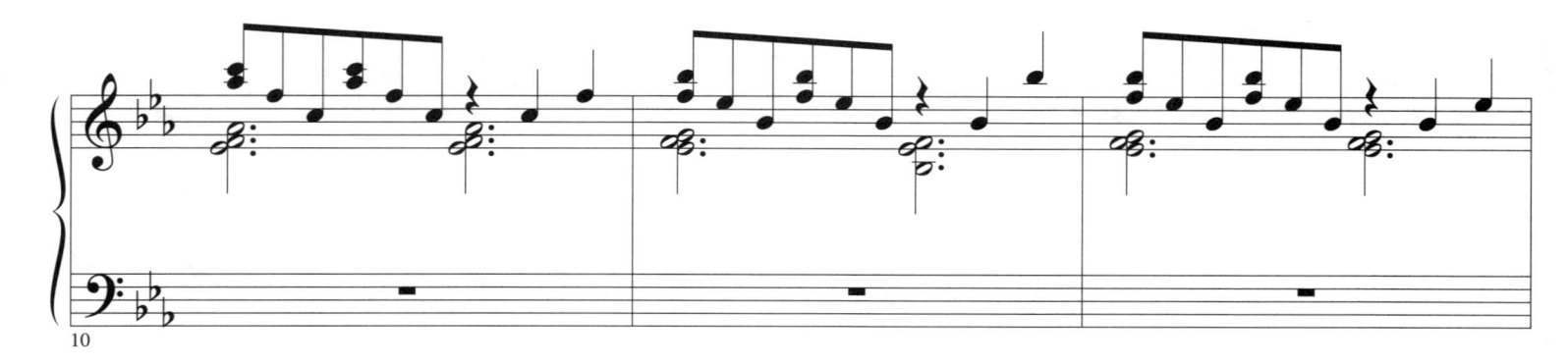

Lightly, in two (♩. = ca. 70)

© Copyright 1978 Maranatha! Music (admin. The Copyright Co., Nashville, TN).
All Rights Reserved. Used by Permission.

EVEN IF YOU POSSESS A CCLI LICENSE YOU CANNOT COPY ANY MUSIC FROM THIS BOOK.
If you have questions about CCLI, please call 800 / 234-2446.

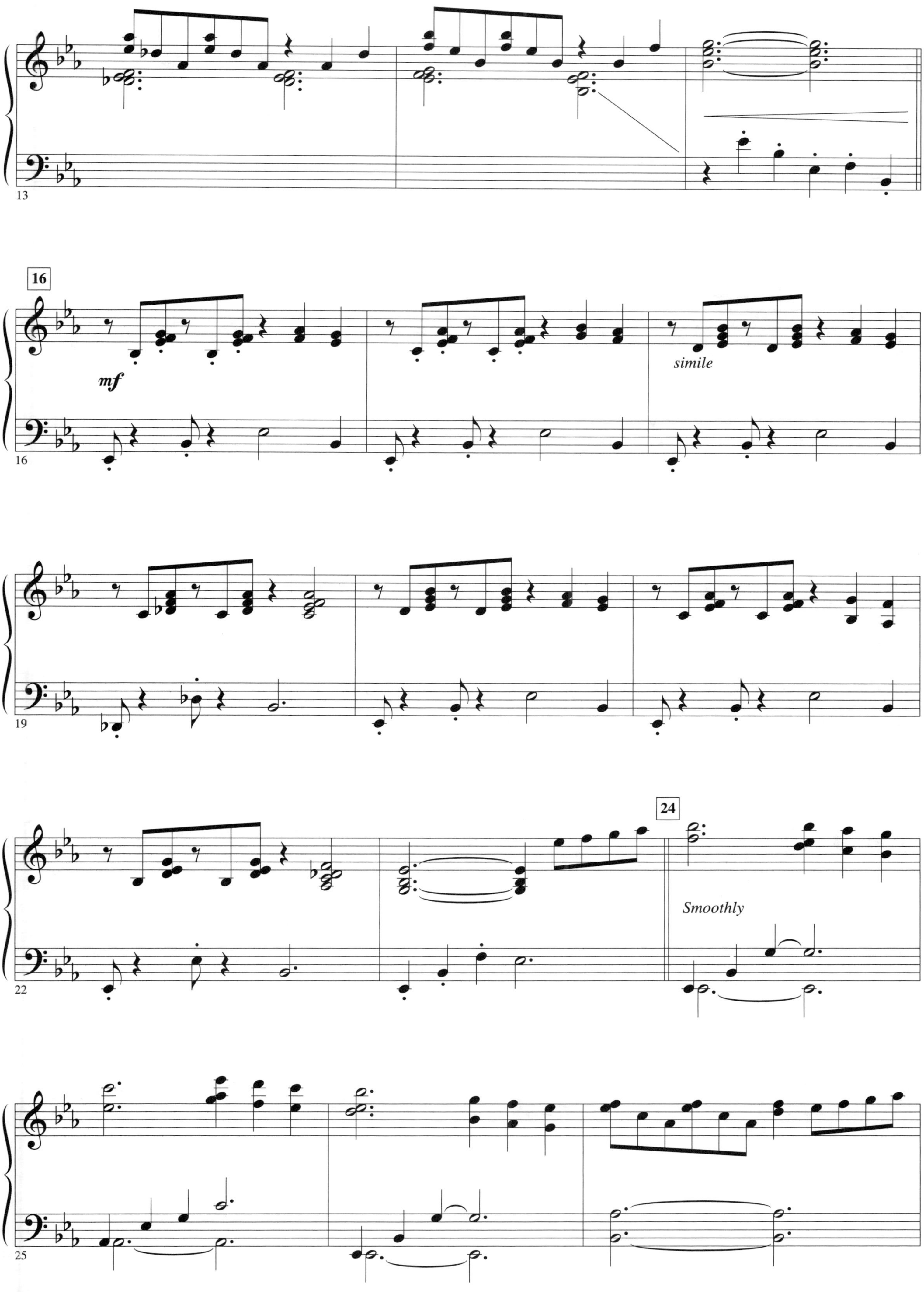
13
16
mf
simile
16
19
22
24
Smoothly
25

O HOW I LOVE JESUS
(Whitfield/Traditional American melody)

Arr. © Copyright 1995 Maranatha! Music (admin. The Copyright Co., Nashville, TN). All Rights Reserved. Used by Permission.

95

(8va)
57
(8va)
59
(8va)
61
slight accel.
Slightly faster (𝅗𝅥. = ca. 68)
64
(8va)
64
(loco)
(Opt. 8va through meas. 72.)
67

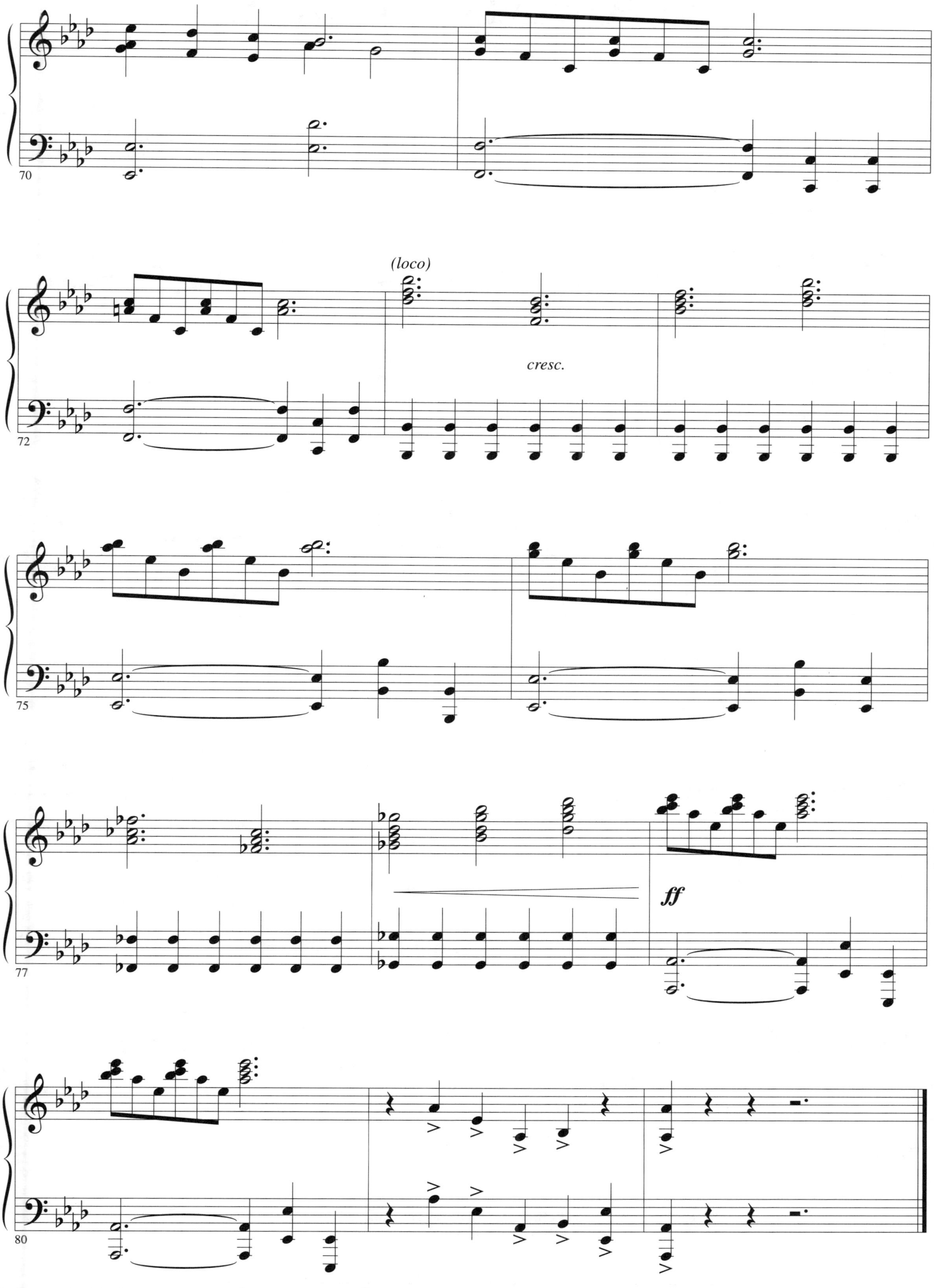
70
72
(loco)
cresc.
75
77
ff
80

You Are My All in All
(Second Keyboard)

Words and Music by
DENNIS JERNIGAN
Orchestrated and arranged by Bruce Greer

Gently (♩ = ca. 63)

"Baroque feel"
mp

simile

© Copyright 1990 Shepherd's Heart Music, Inc. (admin. by Dayspring Music, Inc.)/BMI.
All Rights Reserved. Used by Permission.

EVEN IF YOU POSSESS A **CCLI** LICENSE YOU CANNOT COPY ANY MUSIC FROM THIS BOOK.
If you have questions about CCLI, please call 800 / 234-2446.

99

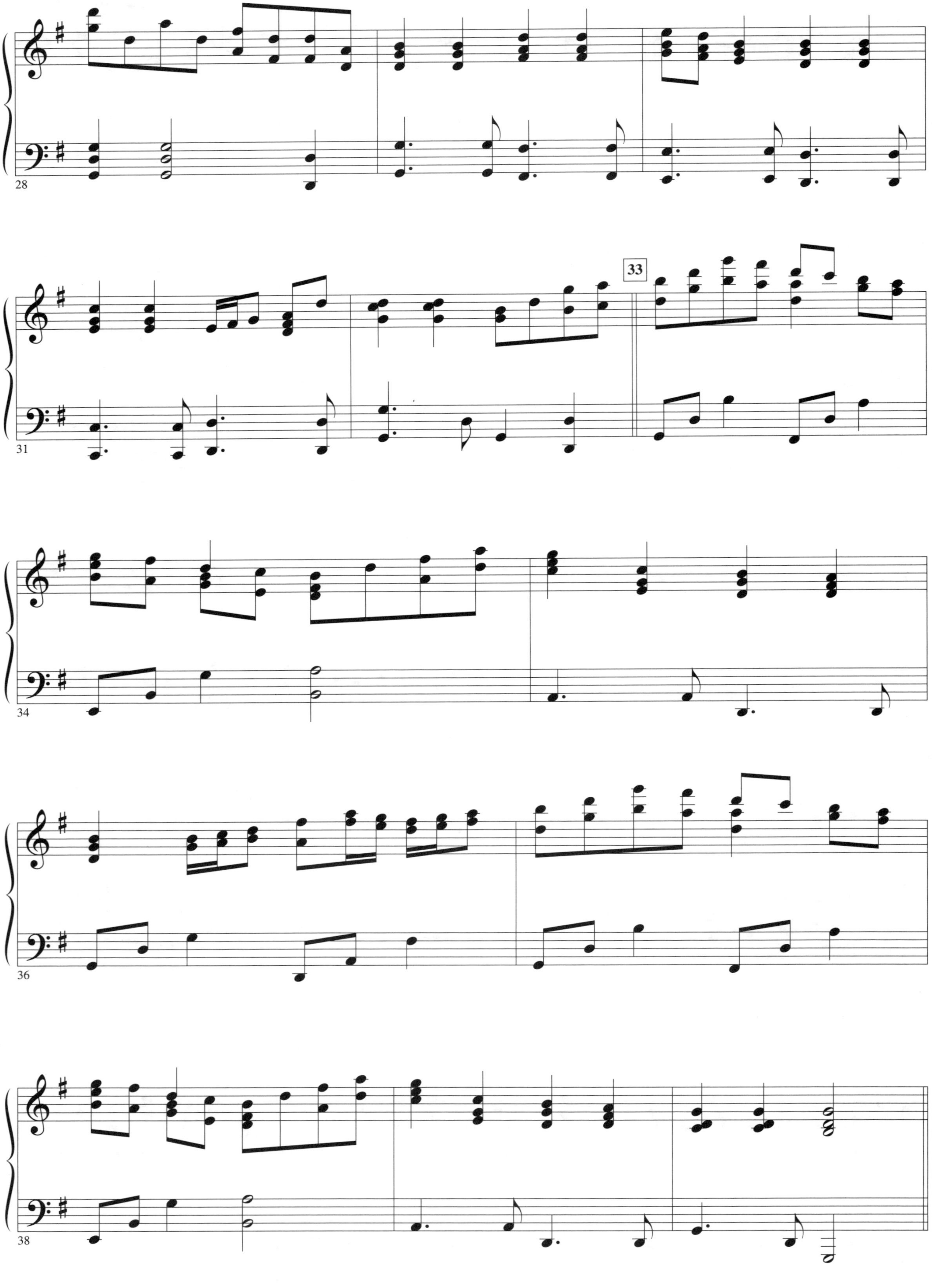
28
31
33
34
36
38

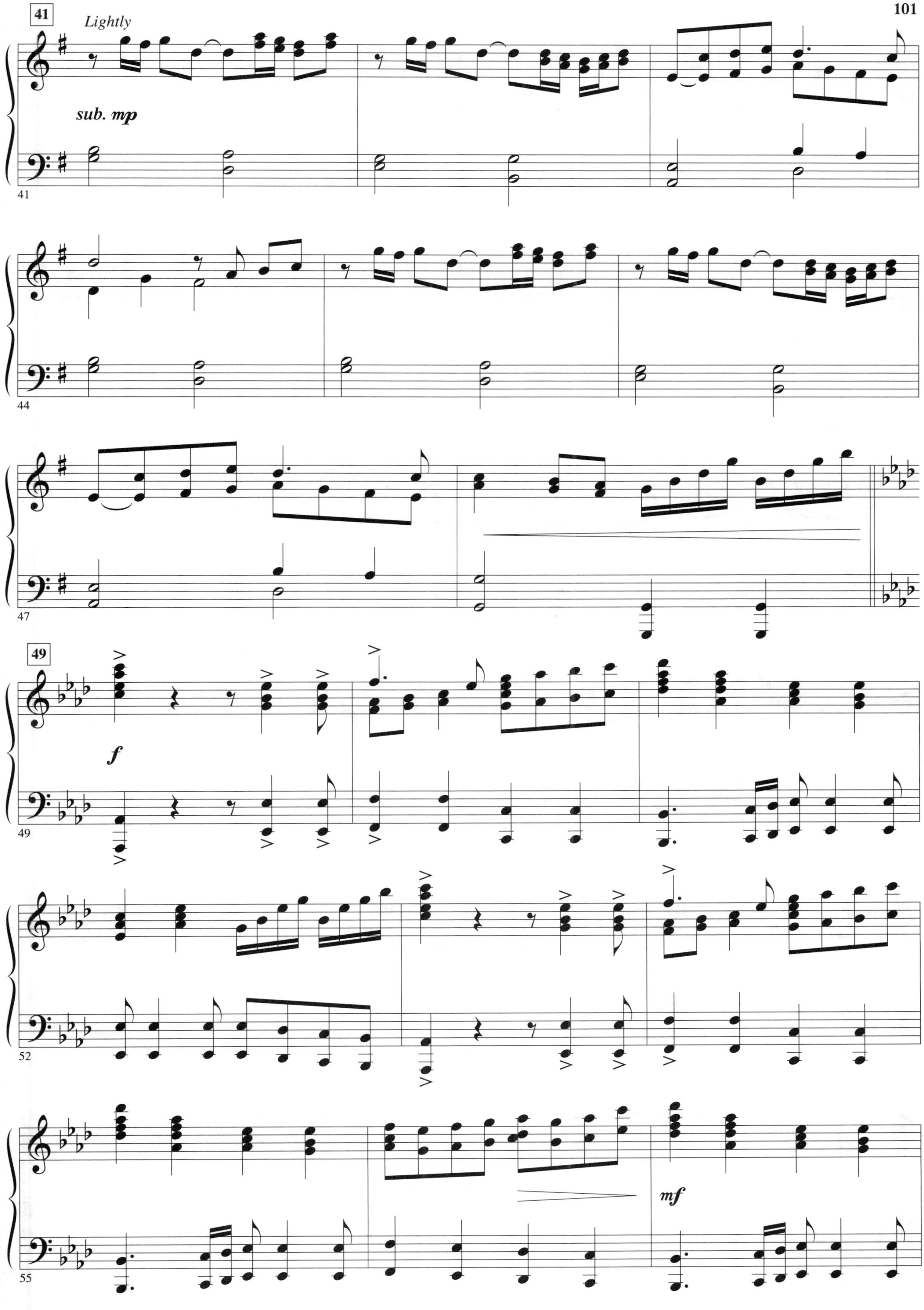
41
Lightly
sub. mp
41
44
47
49
f
49
52
55
mf

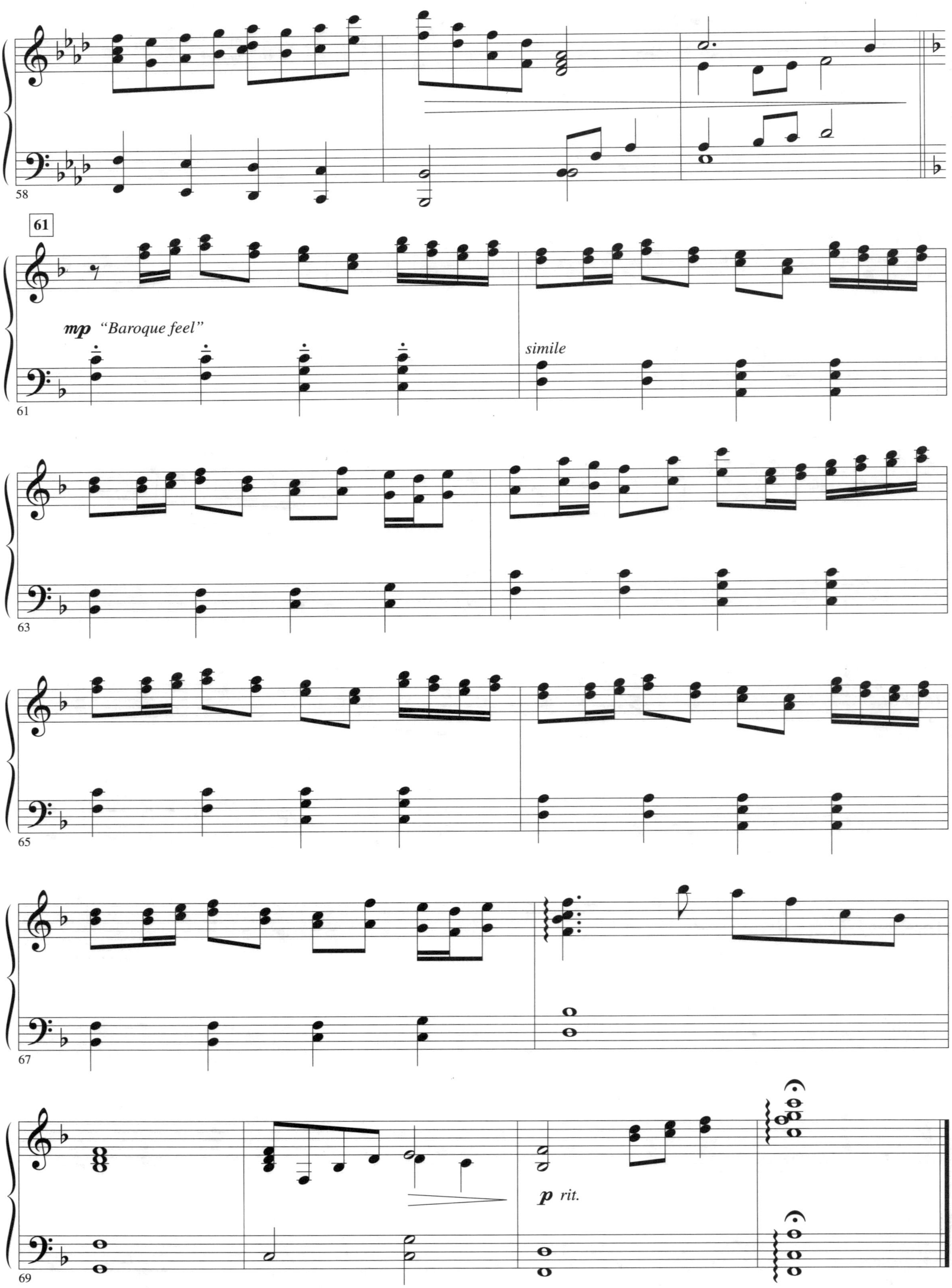
58
61
mp "Baroque feel"
simile
61
63
65
67
p rit.
69

He Is Our Peace

with It Is Well with My Soul

(Second Keyboard)

Words and Music by
KANDELA GROVES
Arranged and orchestrated by Bruce Greer

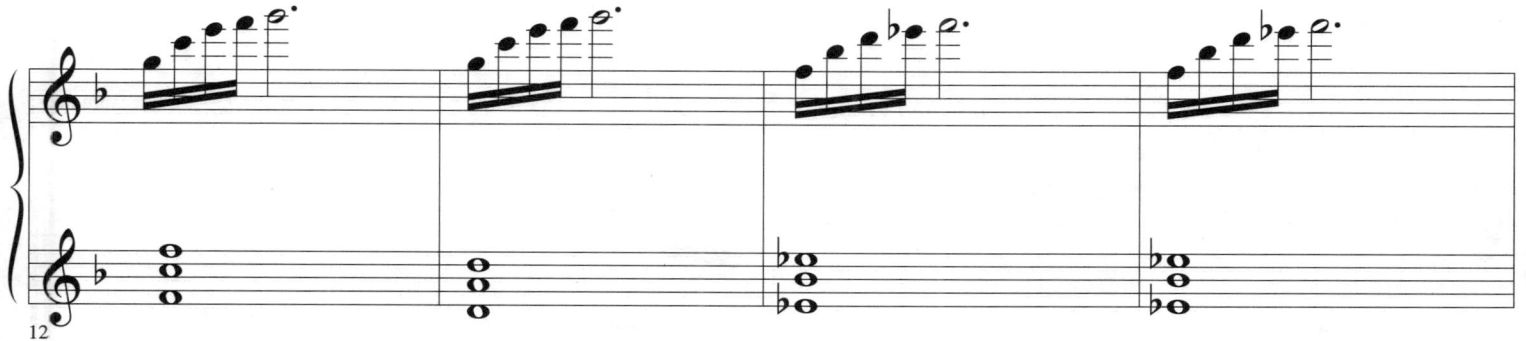

Simply (♩ = ca. 90)

© Copyright 1975 Maranatha! Music (admin. The Copyright Co., Nashville, TN).
All Rights Reserved. Used by Permission.

EVEN IF YOU POSSESS A **CCLI** LICENSE YOU CANNOT COPY ANY MUSIC FROM THIS BOOK.
If you have questions about CCLI, please call 800 / 234-2446.

16
20
23
26
Slightly faster (♩ = 96)
(mf–f)
26
4th time to CODA
1., 3.
(to measure 26.)
30

IT IS WELL WITH MY SOUL (Spafford/Bliss)

Come Just as You Are

(Second Keyboard)

Words and Music by
JOSEPH SABOLICK
Arranged and orchestrated by Bruce Greer

Moderate four ($\quarternote$ = ca. 80)

© Copyright 1994 Maranatha Praise, Inc. (admin. The Copyright Co., Nashville, TN).
All Rights Reserved. Used by Permission.

EVEN IF YOU POSSESS A **CCLI** LICENSE YOU CANNOT COPY ANY MUSIC FROM THIS BOOK.
If you have questions about CCLI, please call 800 / 234-2446.

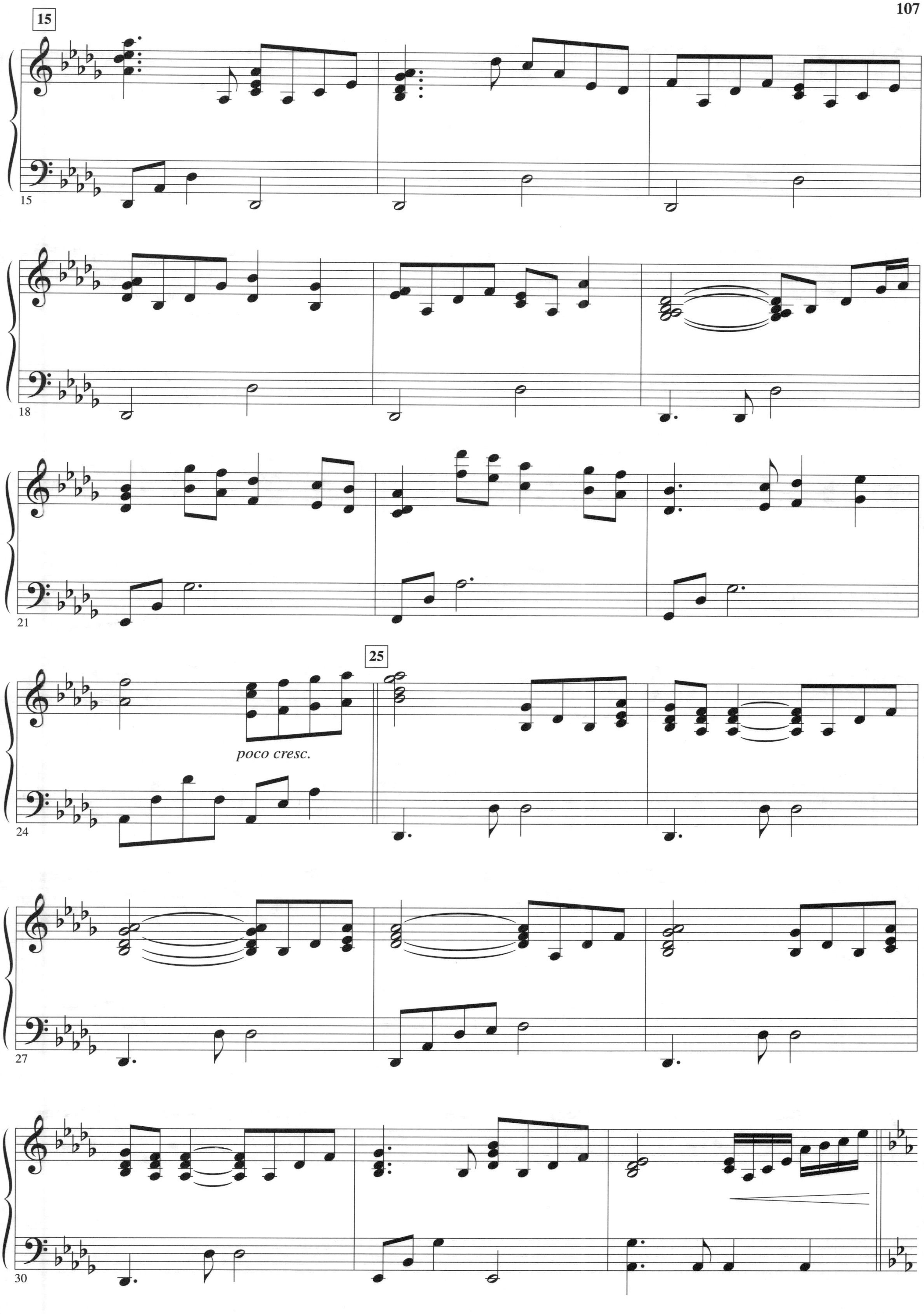
15
15
18
21
25
poco cresc.
24
27
30

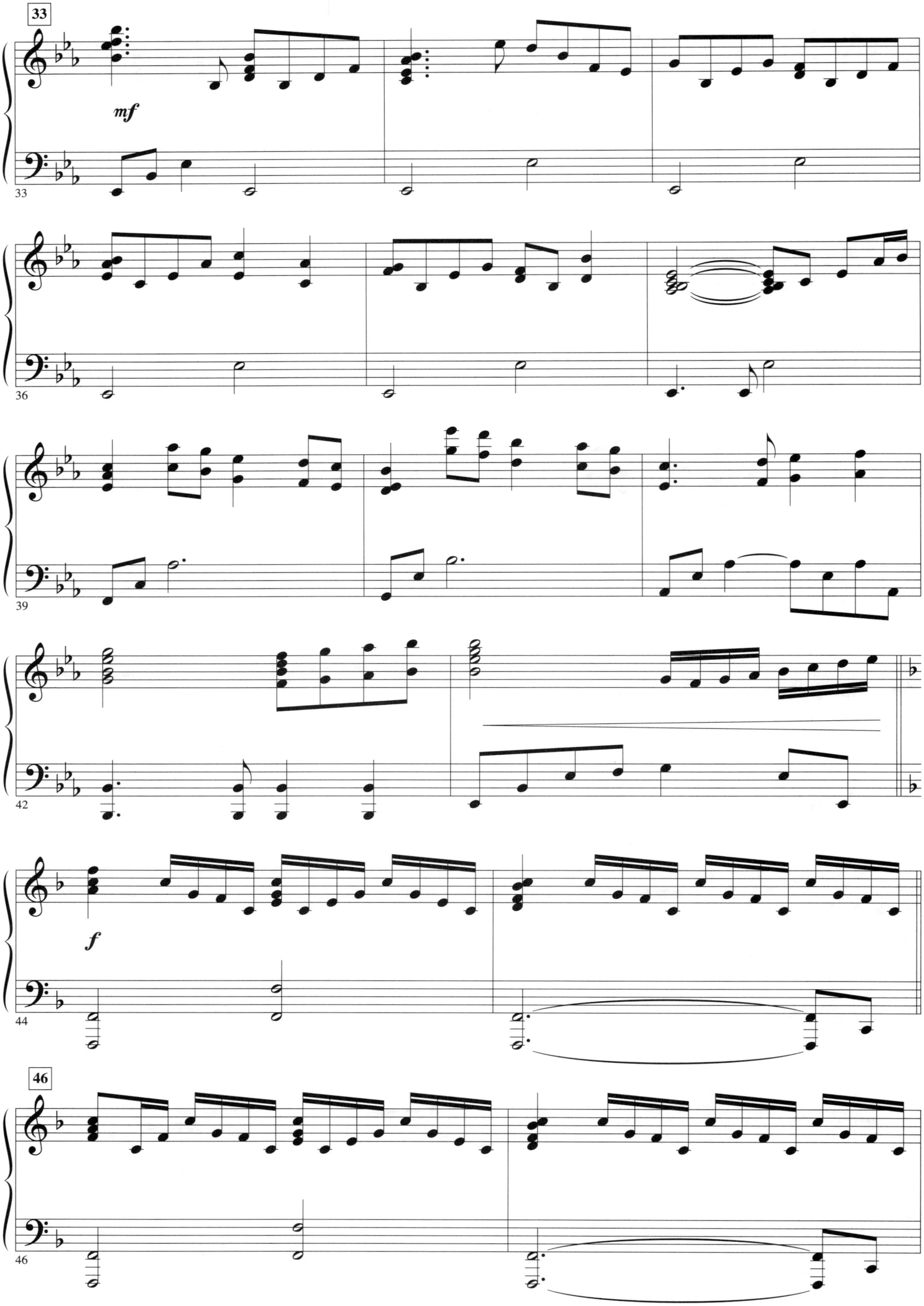
33
mf
33
36
39
42
f
44
46
46

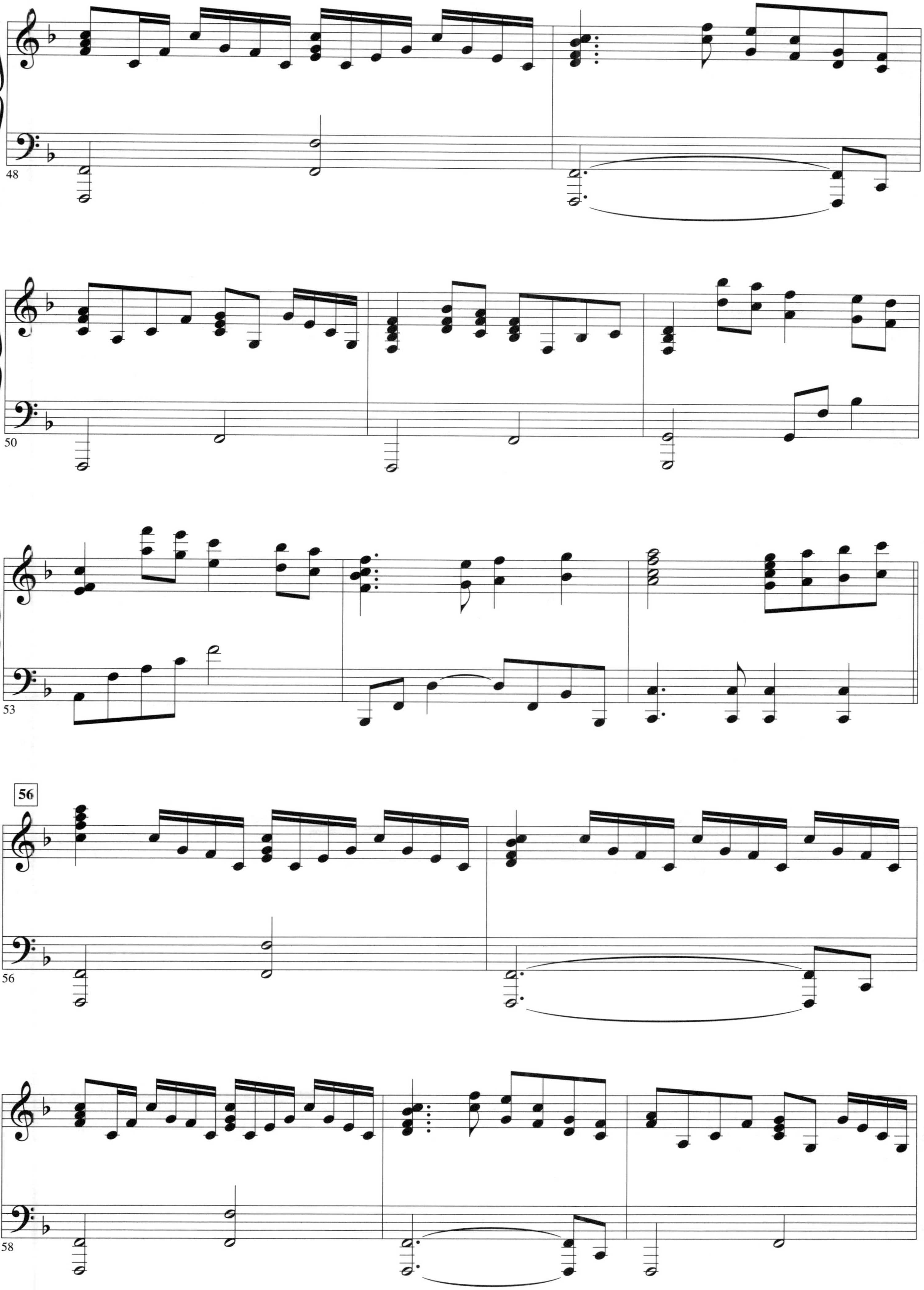
48
50
53
56
56
58

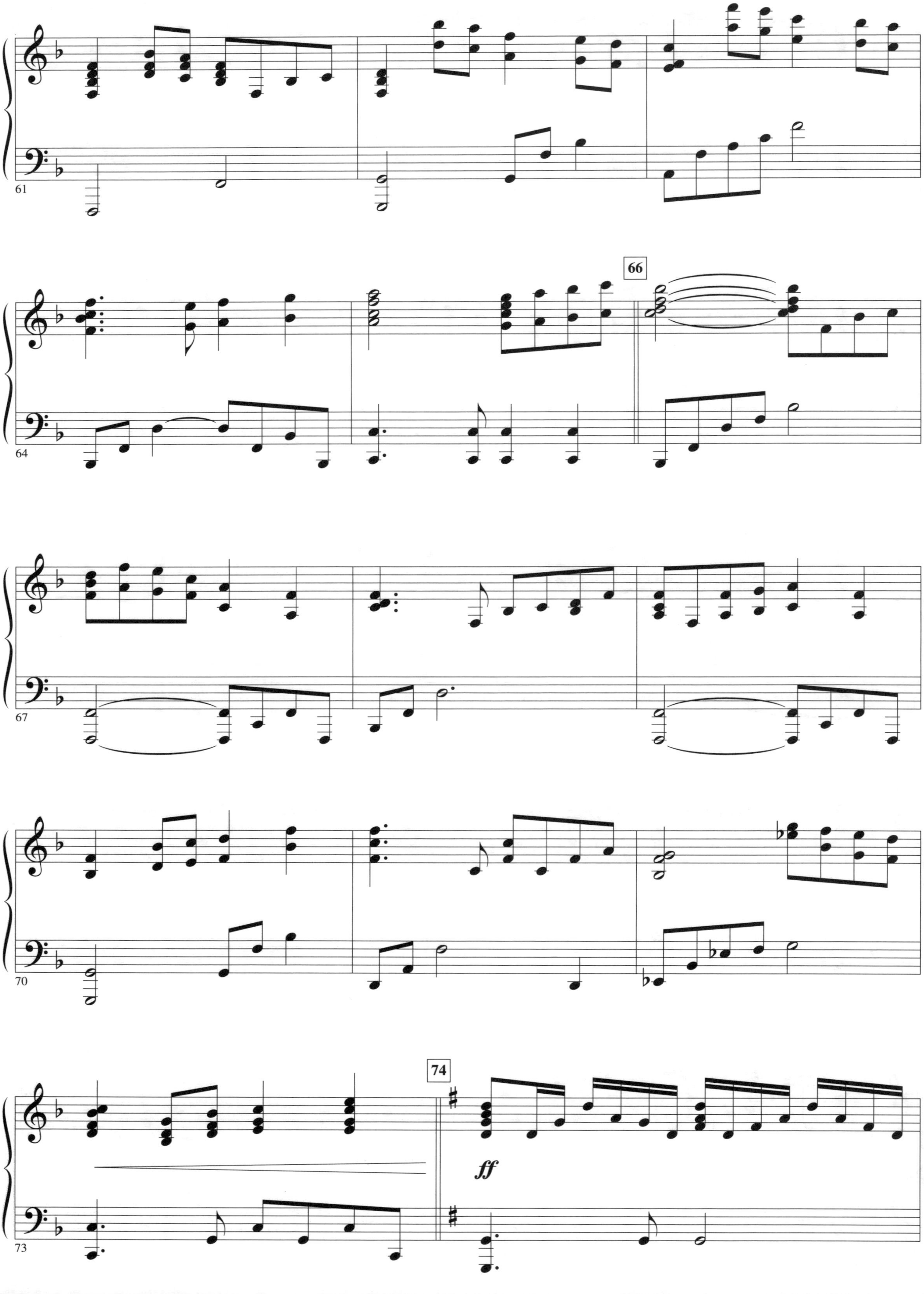
61
64
66
67
70
73
74
ff

111